EAT & EXPLORE Ohio

Cookbook & Travel Guide

Ohio

Cookbook & Travel Guide

by Christy Campbell

Great American Publishers
www.GreatAmericanPublishers.com
TOLL-FREE 1-888-854-5954

Great American Publishers

501 Avalon Way Suite B • Brandon, MS 39047

TOLL-FREE 1-888-854-5954 • www.GreatAmericanPublishers.com

ISBN 978-1-934817-22-3

10 9 8 7 6 5 4 3

by Christy Campbell

Front cover: Map ©The National Atlas of the United States of America • Compass ©thinkstock/istock/scanrail • Columbus ©thinkstock/istock/Long_Strange_Trip_01 • Grand Rapids Applebutter Fest, Zanesville-Muskingum County Convention and Visitors Bureau Back cover: Hocking Hills Tourism Association • Cookies ©istock/Demansia Chapter opening photos: Appetizers & Beverages © Smokingdrum/istockphoto.com • Bread & Breakfast ©Tannjuska/thinkstock.com • Soups & Salads ©funwithfood/istockphoto.com • Vegetables & Other Side Dishes ©Diana Didyk/istockphoto.com • Meat & Seafood ©Ezhicheg/istockphoto.com • Desserts & Other Sweets ©Edward ONeil Photography/istockphoto.com • Index ©thinkstock/istock/vikiri Page photos: background ©thinkstock/istock/DavidMSchrader • striped napkin ©thinkstock/hemera/Liubov Shirokova • map and compass ©thinkstock/istock/scanrail • p1 Columbus ©thinkstock/istock/Long_Strange_Trip_01 • p2 Barn in eastern Ohio ©thinkstock/nikonphotog • p3 map ©The National Atlas of the United States of America, Columbus ©thinkstock/istock/Long_Strange_Trip_01 p6 Cleveland ©thinkstock/Stone-Photos • • p22 Marisa's Salsa ©thinkstock/istock/ bhofack2 • p26 Bacon Wrapped Water Chestnuts ©thinkstock/Purestock • p32 Easy Pretzel Bites ©thinkstock/istock/ kzenon • p38 Green Smoothie ©thinkstock/istock/Lecic • p39 Common Ground Canopy Tours ©thinkstock/istock/Ammit • p44 Cherry Bounce ©thinkstock/istock/RealCG Animation Studio • p48 Cornbread ©thinkstock/istock/AbbieImages • p50 Apricot White Chocolate Bread ©thinkstock/istock/Lesyy • p54 Pumpkin Bread ©thinkstock/istock/Ildiko Papp • p60 Raisin Bran Muffins ©thinkstock/istock/Lew Robertson • p66 Whole Grain Pancakes ©thinkstock/istock/Elena Elisseeva • p67 Asian Boat Fest ©thinkstock/istock/shih-wei • p74 Bacon Egg Lasagna ©thinkstock/istock/Siraphol • p92 Tomato Soup ©thinkstock/istock/MinnaRossi • p102 White Chicken Chili ©thinkstock/istock/StephanieFrey • p114 Buffalo Chicken Salad ©thinkstock/istock/Shaiith • p116 Buttermilk Coleslaw/Ribs ©thinkstock/istock/paulbinet • p135 Mushroom Casserole ©istock/tarczas • p138 Oscar's Vegetable Casserole ©thinkstock/istock/Margaret Edwards • p142 Glazed Carrots ©thinkstock/istock/supercat67 • p146 Broccoli Casserole ©thinkstock/istock/Stephanie Frey • p152 Meatballs ©thinkstock/istock/papkin • p168 Chicken Enchiladas ©thinkstock/istock/travelling-light • p170 Chicken Cutlets ©thinkstock/istock/runin • p220 Strawberry Mousse ©thinkstock/istock/Pugovica88 • p221 Newark Strawberry Festival ©thinkstock/moodboard • p228 Buckeyes ©istock/jatrax

Contents

STATES POST OFFICE

Introduction

I have spent countless hours absorbing state facts for the Eat & Explore State Cookbook Series. Each state has a unique fingerprint in the history of this great country, and Ohio's beautiful landscape and rich heritage bring it to the forefront of states to be explored. Living in the central part of Mississippi, I am fairly landlocked, and I am intrigued by the northernmost border of Ohio's amazing lakefront. Central Mississippi is also home to tall pines and the landscape of gorgeous, green-leafed buckeye trees painting the patchwork of Ohio is indeed a departure from what I am accustomed. The Buckeye State is a fascinating place, and I imagine America's early explorers traversing the banks of the grand lakefront, traipsing through hills and valleys, and staking their claim. As I unfolded Ohio piece by piece, the answer of why this state is beloved by many became apparent; Ohio's plentiful resources, stunning scenery, and a love of community that is filled with state pride makes Ohio a special place in the heart of America.

My passage of discovery through "The Mother of Presidents" heralds a vision of warm kitchens and joyous family gatherings. This vision includes the scent of warm cinnamon from a baking cake, farmhouse dinner tables with fresh bread, and the sights and smells of celebrations and delicious food filling the air of hometown festivals. ***Potato Soup***, ***Bloody Mary Tomatoes***, ***Apricot White Chocolate Bread***, and ***Basil and Bell Pepper Pesto*** are local favorites welcome at every meal. The deliciousness continues with ***The Inn's Signature Smoked Salmon Seven-Cheese Frittata***, ***Herb Stuffed Pork Chops***, ***Irish Beef Stew***, and ***Pumpkin Muffins***. However, the most loved section of any cookbook for many people is the dessert chapter, and *Eat & Explore Ohio* does not disappoint. ***Creamy Peach Pie***, ***Chocolate Chip Cheesecake***, ***Popcorn Cake***, and ***Red Velvet Whoopies*** are decadent desserts deserving of trying again and again!

This latest addition to the EAT & EXPLORE STATE COOKBOOK SERIES takes our team further into the country's family celebrations and traditions. Great American Publishers is growing by leaps and bounds, and each project needs a great team to make it a reality. Our team is truly exceptional, and these great women take on tasks and achieve milestones not to be ignored. Brooke Craig, Diane Rothery, Anita Musgrove (author *Back Road Restaurant Recipes*), Tory Hackett, Krista Griffin, Amber Feiock, Sheree Smith, and Pam Edwards take every endeavor to the next level

I want to give special recognition to several people who were vital to the creation of *Eat & Explore Ohio*. Christy Kent took the reins, ensuring that *Eat & Explore Ohio* would be a great addition to our library. Cyndi Clark gave it panache, and Sheila and Roger Simmons made sure it came to fruition. I am forever grateful for these smart and talented people, without them this book would not have been complete.

The EAT & EXPLORE STATE COOKBOOK SERIES has been a part of my family for the past 5 years. My boisterous son Preston sits by my side while I edit and write. My inquisitive son Michael reads everything he can, and I love turning my finished books over for him to pour over. My husband Michael's unending support, patience, and unwavering strength has made it possible for me to complete yet another book.

The tremendous state of Ohio is the latest stop on our journey across American. The Buckeye State is now a permanent fixture in my heart, and I hope it lands in the reader's hearts as well. So take a seat, buckle in, and let's get on to exploring…Ohio.

Appetizers &
Beverages

Hummus

1 (15-ounce) can chickpeas, drained
2 tablespoons olive oil
⅓ cup lemon juice
1 clove garlic
¼ cup sesame seed oil (tahini)
1 teaspoon salt
Paprika for garnish

Rinse chickpeas. Skins can be removed by rubbing the peas between your fingers. This will make a smoother hummus. Put peas in blender, add oil, lemon juice, garlic, tahini and salt. Blend until smooth. Refrigerate until ready to serve. Garnish with paprika.

Vermilion Valley Vineyards

Vermilion Valley Vineyards

11005 Gore Orphanage Road • Wakeman, OH 44889
440-965-5202 • www.vermilionvalleyvineyards.com

Vermilion Valley Vineyards is a small, owner operated winery situated on a 23-acre rural property located about 10 miles south of Lake Erie's southern shore. Their grape wines include more than a dozen premium types produced from plantings of classic varieties such as Cabernet franc, Chardonnay, and Riesling. The rustic, award winning winery building that houses a tasting room and the beautiful landscapes make a superb venue for individuals and entire families seeking an intimate encounter with nature and a chance to witness environmentally friendly agricultural land-use practices.

Light foods are routinely available, and more substantial fare can be enjoyed during weekend events such as clambakes and harvest time dinners. Live entertainment is a regular feature during Friday and Saturday evenings. The picturesque events pavilion overlooking a beautifully vegetated wetland is particularly well suited for weddings and reunions. Please visit their website for information about hours, location, rental opportunities, and wines.

White Bean Hummus

1 (10-ounce) can beans (garbanzo beans, butter beans)
1 garlic clove, crushed
2 to 3 tablespoons The Olive Scene Sicilian Lemon Balsamic Vinegar
1 tablespoon water
1 pinch red pepper flakes
1 pinch salt
4 basil leaves
1 tablespoon The Olive Scene Chipotle Olive Oil
Crudités (spears of vegetables of your choice)

In a food processor, add all ingredients, except crudités, and process until very smooth. Add a couple drops of water if too thick. Arrange crudités on a plate with a bowl of hummus for dipping.

The Olive Scene

Baked Artichoke Hearts

16 ounces Parmesan cheese
16 ounces Italian-style breadcrumbs
¼ cup canola oil
1 tablespoon garlic powder
1 tablespoon basil
1 tablespoon oregano
1 (14-ounce) can artichoke hearts
1 egg
1 cup milk

Combine cheese, breadcrumbs, oil and spices. Mix thoroughly. Cut artichoke hearts into quarters. Combine egg and milk in shallow bowl. Dip artichoke heart quarters in egg and milk mixture and roll in cheese and breadcrumb mixture. Place in lightly greased shallow baking dish. Bake in 350° oven 20 to 25 minutes or until golden brown.

Hocking Hills Tourism Association

Cheddar Fondue

¼ cup butter
¼ cup flour
Salt and pepper to taste
¼ teaspoon ground mustard
¼ teaspoon Worcestershire sauce
1½ cups milk
8 ounces shredded Cheddar cheese
Bread cubes
Ham cubes
Bite-size sausage and/or broccoli florets

In saucepan melt butter, stir in flour, salt, pepper, mustard and Worcestershire sauce until smooth. Gradually add milk. Bring to a boil; cook and stir until thickened; reduce heat. Add cheese; cook and stir until melted. Transfer to fondue pot or slow cooker; keep warm. Serve with bread, ham, sausage and/or broccoli.

Gertrude Rasor
Columbus Park of Roses

Pumpkin Cream Cheese Dip

1 (8-ounce) package Neufchâtel cream cheese, softened
1 cup plain fat-free Greek yogurt
¾ cup canned pumpkin
½ cup powdered sugar
½ teaspoon cinnamon
4 to 5 apples, cored and sliced
Additional cinnamon, apple sticks and graham cracker sticks for garnish

Place cream cheese in a medium mixing bowl. Using a hand mixer beat cream cheese until smooth. Add yogurt and pumpkin, mix until smooth. Add powdered sugar and cinnamon, mix until incorporated. Place in serving bowl and refrigerate until serving. Garnish with a couple shakes of cinnamon and serve with apple slices or graham cracker sticks.

Erin Black
Leaders Farm

Vidalia Onion Dip

¾ cup Cooper's Vidalia Onion Relish
1 (8-ounce) block cream cheese, softened

Blend relish and cream cheese together. Refrigerate 4 hours before serving. Store in refrigerator. Great on vegetables, crackers, bagels, or as a sandwich spread.

Cooper's Mill Apple Butter & Jelly Factory

Cooper's Mill

Apple Butter & Jelly Factory

1414 North Sandusky Avenue
Bucyrus, OH 44820
419-562-4215
www.coopers-mill.com

At Cooper's Mill, there is great pride in making the homemade jams, jellies, fruit butters and relishes that people have come to know and love for the past 45 years. These all-natural products are made in small batches using recipes that have been passed down for generations. There are never any artificial colors, sweeteners or preservatives used; only simple, natural ingredients go into every jar. Guests are invited to tour our factory in Bucyrus, Ohio to see just how delicious ripe fruits are transformed into irresistible products that are sure to please. After the tour, guests are welcomed to stop by the newly-remodeled market and gift shop to sample and purchase tasty treats and more. The marketplace is open year-round and also features a growing selection of Amish meats and cheeses, local foods, seasonal produce, fresh-baked goods, homemade fudge, specialty gifts and more. Experience the simple goodness of Cooper's Mill today!

Cincinnati Chili-Cheese Dip

1 (8-ounce) package cream cheese, softened
13 to 15 ounces Cincinnati-style chili
8 ounces shredded Cheddar cheese

Spread softened cream cheese evenly on bottom of an 8x8-inch baking pan. Layer heated chili over cream cheese. Top evenly with Cheddar. Heat in 350° oven 10 minutes. Let stand 5 to 10 minutes before serving with corn chips or tortilla chips.

American Sign Museum

EXPLORE

American Sign Museum

1330 Monmouth Street • Cincinnati, OH 45225
513-541-6366 • www.signmuseum.org

Wednesday through Saturday 10am to 4pm • Sunday 12pm to 4pm
Guided Tour Times:
Wednesday through Saturday 11am and 2pm • Sunday 2pm
Call or Check Website for Winter and Summer Tour Schedules

The American Sign Museum is a journey through a half century of sign history, beginning with the fancy gold leaf glass signs of the early 1900s, through the pre-neon era of light bulb signs, to neon's heyday in the 1930s to 1940s, and on into the plastic era of the funky '50s. There are spinning sputnik-like signs from the Jetsons period, and handlettered showcards from the Las Vegas days of Frank Sinatra and Charo. Visitors will learn about neon—how it works and how different colors are achieved. Family, friends and groups will enjoy a fun and educational experience. During the weekdays, visits often include a neon demonstration provided by Neonworks—a commercial neon shop located inside the museum.

Awesome Taco Dip

1 pound Bob Evans Hot n' Zesty Sausage, browned and drained
1 (10-ounce) can Rotel diced tomatoes and green chiles
1 (8-ounce) package cream cheese, softened

Combine all ingredients together in small slow cooker on low until melted together. Serve with pita chips

Ashland Balloonfest

Shrimp Puff

2 cups Monterey Jack cheese, shredded
2 cups Monterey Jack with peppers, shredded
10 eggs
½ cup flour
1 teaspoon baking powder
¼ teaspoon salt
2 cups cottage cheese
½ cup butter, melted
3 green onions, chopped
1 teaspoon each thyme, tarragon, basil
1 (7-ounce) can mushrooms, drained and chopped
1 (6-ounce) can tiny shrimp, drained

Preheat oven to 400°. Grease a 10x13-inch casserole dish. Combine Monterey Jack cheeses together and divide in half; set aside. In a large bowl, beat eggs, flour, baking powder, salt, cottage cheese and butter. Fold in half of cheeses and all remaining ingredients. Place mixture in greased casserole. Sprinkle with remaining cheese and bake 20 minutes or until golden and puffy. Cut into small squares and serve warm.

Fitzgerald's Irish Bed & Breakfast

Empanadas

2 pounds ground chuck, browned and drained
1 (12-ounce) package frozen onions
1 (12-ounce) package frozen green bell peppers
1 tablespoon fresh minced garlic
1 tablespoon oregano
1 (8-ounce) can tomato sauce
1 cup beer
1 cup sliced green olives
1 egg
½ cup water
24 empanada shells or 24 wonton wrappers*

Combine browned beef and all ingredients except egg, water and shells in stockpot. Cook over medium heat, uncovered, 2 to 3 hours stirring occasionally. Combine egg and water in small pastry dish. Place a spoonful of empanada meat mixture in center of shell. Brush edges of shell with egg wash. Fold over and be sure edges are sealed with egg wash. Fill deep-fry pan three-quarters full with canola oil. Heat to 350°. Drop empanadas into hot oil and cook, flipping once, until golden brown. Remove from fry pan to paper bag for good oil draining. Serve with salsa and/or sour cream.

*Empanada shells can usually be found at a Cuban grocery store. Wonton wrappers can be substituted, which are available in your grocer's freezer.

Hocking Hills Tourism Association

Stuffed Mushrooms with Blue Cheese

2 dozen large mushrooms
¼ cup sliced green onions
1 clove garlic, minced
¼ cup butter, melted
⅔ cup fine dry breadcrumbs
½ cup crumbled blue cheese

Preheat oven to 425°. Wash and drain mushrooms. Remove stems. Chop enough stems to make 1 cup. In a medium saucepan cook stems, onion and garlic in butter until tender. Stir in breadcrumbs and cheese. Spoon crumb mixture into mushroom caps. Arrange mushrooms in a baking pan. Bake 8 to 10 minutes or until heated through.

The Alpacas of Spring Acres

Lump Crab Salsa

3 tablespoons chopped cilantro
2 medium shallots, chopped
1 red bell pepper, diced
1 jalapeño, seeded and diced
Zest and juice of 1 lime
1 garlic clove, diced
¼ cup olive oil
2 pounds lump crabmeat
Salt and pepper to taste
½ cup salted and roasted almonds, chopped

In a large bowl, combine cilantro, shallots, bell pepper, jalapeño, lime zest, lime juice, garlic and olive oil. Fold in crabmeat and season with salt and pepper. Refrigerate 1 hour. Remove from refrigerator and let salsa come to room temperature and fold in almonds just before serving. Serve with chips.

Grove City Town Center Wine and Arts Festival

Grove City Mistletoe Market

First Saturday in December

3378 Park Street • Grove City, OH 43123
614-539-8762

Grove City's charming Mistletoe Market, offers its youth Secret Santa services to assist in independent purchases. Fine crafters, sweet treats, and hot holiday foods fill the heated Grand Tent, selected City Hall rooms, and various Town Center businesses. Experience the parade, Santa's reindeer, seasonal music, and ice sculpting.

EXPLORE

Grove City Town Center Wine and Arts Festival

Third Saturday in June

Park and Broadway
Grove City, OH 43123
614-539-8762
www.grovecitytowncenter.org

Thinking wine? Then drink in Grove City Town Center's annual Wine and Art's Festival, where Ohio's wineries are plentiful and pleasant. Tasters numbering over 30,000, from connoisseur to casually curious, agree that this is the venue for finding favorite vintages! Enjoy the natural complement of wine with art.

Marisa's Salsa

This can be hot but you can back off on the hot peppers.

5 to 6 medium tomatoes
1 green bell pepper
1 sweet red bell pepper
1 hot pepper
1 jalapeño pepper
1 red onion
4 cloves garlic, minced
Juice of 2 lemons
½ cup cilantro, chopped
1 teaspoon sea salt

In a food processor, pulse chop all ingredients to desired consistency.

Larry Slocum, Oxford Farmer's Market

Oxford Kinetics Festival

April

Miami University • Millett Assembly Hall • Oxford, OH 45056
513-461-3096 • www.oxfordkineticsfestival.org

Dust off the monster bike, kit out the catapult, and suit up in the finest mechanical sculpture. Scope out the kinetic art exhibitions, enjoy the many kids activities, fire off some rockets, and munch on great eats. Join in the mayhem every April in Oxford, Ohio.

Ann's Raspberry Farm Brussels Sprout Relish Pinwheels

These can be made in the morning, which makes entertaining simple.

1 (8-ounce) package cream cheese, softened
¼ cup Good Food Award-Winning Savory Brussels Sprout Relish
4 large flour tortillas
4 to 8 thin slices ham or salami or prosciutto
Finely chopped seeded tomato or finely shredded carrots, optional

Blend the cream cheese and relish well. Spread each tortilla with one quarter of the mixture and top with 1 or 2 thin slices of deli meat. It is nice to use a variety. Add an option of your choice for color, if you would like. Roll up the tortillas and slice into ½-inch pinwheels. Chill until serving. Makes 28 pinwheels.

Ann's Raspberry Farm

Ann's Raspberry Farm

'Creating Edible Art from Seed to Jar'

6645 Blair Road
Fredericktown, OH 43019
740-694-1935
www.annsraspberryfarm.com

May through December
8am to 5pm
Monday through Friday

Ann's Raspberry Farm is a Certified Naturally Grown family farm located in the rolling countryside of central Ohio's Amish country. It was founded in 2004 by Daniel and Ann Trudel, who had discovered the area while on their honeymoon. Serendipitously they returned to stay and raise their two children, Eric and Ali, and begin a successful family farming adventure. Falling asleep to the smell of Chocolate Raspberry Jam is among the fondest memories of their children growing up on the farm.

Winners of multiple 'Good Food Awards' for tasty, authentic and responsibly made products and 'Central Ohio Signature Food Award', they feature: Savory Brussels Sprout Relish, Petite Pickled Sprouts, Red Raspberry Jam, Jalapeno Raspberry Jam, Chocolate Raspberry Jam, Hungarian Hot Pepper Mustard and Hot Pepper Jelly. Each of these 'Artisan from Seed to Jar' creations are crafted, exclusively, from their own chemical-free harvest.

Bacon-Wrapped Water Chestnuts

1 cup packed brown sugar
1 tablespoon Worcestershire sauce
2 cups ketchup
2 (8-ounce) cans water chestnuts
1 pound bacon, each slice halved
Toothpicks

Combine sugar, Worcestershire sauce and ketchup; mix well and set aside. Wrap 1 water chestnut with bacon half and secure with toothpick. Repeat. Place in 9x13-inch baking dish. Bake at 375° for 10 minutes. Remove from oven and drain fat. Pour ketchup mixture over wraps and bake an additional 30 minutes.

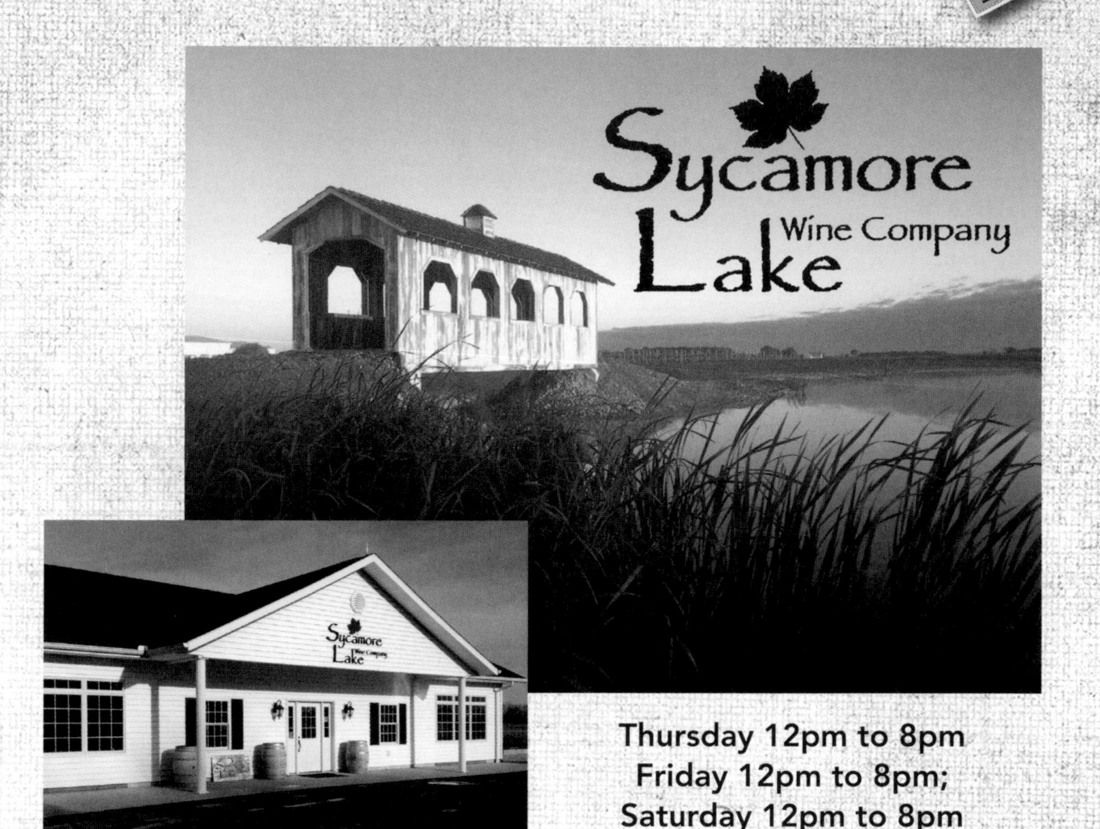

Thursday 12pm to 8pm
Friday 12pm to 8pm;
Saturday 12pm to 8pm

9660 Mayberry Road • Columbus Grove, OH 45830
419-233-1581 • www.sycamorelakewineco.wix.com/winery

Jeff and Janice Hanneman opened Sycamore Lake Wine Company in October 2013, with the tremendous effort of family and friends. They strive to offer a memorable experience through great service and great wine. They are committed to making exceptional Ohio wines and feature a nice selection of red and white wines, from sweet to dry made on premises by Jeff. They also offer a nice variety of appetizers that pair well their wines. While enjoying a glass of wine, browse through the gift area for that unique wine themed gift or accessory. Relax in the comfortable tasting room, on the patio, or stroll through the vineyard surrounded by a 17-acre lake and covered bridge.

Bloody Mary Tomatoes

3 tablespoons salt
1 tablespoon pepper
8 small (1½ inches in diameter) ripe tomatoes from the garden
½ to 1 cup vodka or Campari, optional
½ cup Frank's hot sauce
8 ounces cream cheese, softened
2 ounces finely crumbled blue cheese, softened
2 ounces goat cheese, softened
1 tablespoon unsalted butter, softened
4 to 6 tablespoons whipping cream
½ cup baby shrimp
¼ cup sliced olives
2 slices cooked bacon, finely chopped
½ cup chopped parsley
16 miniature cupcake liners

In a small dish combine salt and pepper; set aside. Cut each tomato in half and trim uncut side to ensure tomato half sits straight. Fill eye dropper with vodka and insert about 1 teaspoon into center of each tomato. (Omit if making the virgin version.) Brush top side of each tomato with hot sauce. Liberally sprinkle salt and pepper mixture on top of hot sauce. Let set 10 minutes. In the meantime, combine cheeses, butter, whipping cream and a pinch of salt and pepper mixture until smooth. Add more cream if necessary. Place mixture in pastry bag fitted with star-shaped decorating tip. Using pastry bag, carefully pipe approximately 1 to 1½ tablespoons of cheese mixture onto the top of each tomato.

Decorate with shrimp, olives or bacon, then sprinkle with chopped parsley. Place each tomato in a cupcake liner to serve.

Homestead House Bed and Breakfast

Homestead House Bed and Breakfast

38111 West Spaulding Street • Willoughby, OH 44094
440-946-1902 • www.HomesteadHousebb.com

Built in 1884, this award winning Italianate home offers old world charm and hospitality with luxury accommodations with canopy beds, fireplaces and Jacuzzis. Guests can relax on the large front porch, get a massage, or stroll the historic New England style town visiting quaint shops, boutiques and restaurants—but save room for the gourmet three-course breakfast. Located just three miles from Lake Erie beaches, the Holden Arboretum, Morman Historic Center and President Garfield's House, there is something for every interests be it shopping, fishing, hiking or cross country skiing. Enjoy wineries and sample the best Ohio has to offer. Additionally, Homestead House Bed and Breakfast is a short 20 minutes from Cleveland, giving easy access to the Rock and Roll Hall of Fame, Cleveland's theatre and museum district as well as the West Side Market, Cleveland's historic indoor food emporium.

This Trip Advisor five-star award winning B&B is sure to become a favorite Northeast Ohio destination.

The Apple Fest

4th weekend in September

www.newparisapplefest.com

The New Paris Area Chamber of Commerce, Convention & Visitors Bureau is proud to welcome guests to the great "AppleFest" tradition in the village. This three day festival, held on the fourth weekend in September, is chock full of great things to do, eat, see and enjoy. There are plenty of vendors to explore, a great classic car show, rides, food, music and a flea market. Bring the family and discover the fun at the New Paris AppleFest. New Paris truly is "A village for all seasons"...

New Paris, OH

www.newparisoh.com

Nestled in the beautiful rural countryside of Preble County and surrounded by rolling hills, the Village of New Paris is a friendly and charming place to visit. With great places to enjoy a meal with friends, after shopping for antiques, or buying fresh apples and pies from the nearby orchard, they have everything that makes small town living enjoyable.

Easy Pretzel Bites

- 1 (.75-ounce) package dry active yeast
- 1½ cups warm water
- ¾ tablespoon sugar
- 4 cups all-purpose flour
- ½ teaspoon salt
- 1 large egg
- Coarse salt
- 4 tablespoons unsalted butter, melted

Preheat oven to 425°. Line a baking sheet with parchment paper. In a large bowl, combine yeast and warm water and allow yeast to dissolve. Add sugar to yeast mixture and stir till dissolved. Add flour and salt; mix well. Turn dough onto a floured board and knead until smooth. It is best of add flour to your hands before kneading so the dough does not stick. In a separate bowl, beat egg and set aside. Divide dough into 5 sections. Roll each section into long rope-shaped pieces, about 1 inch in diameter. Cut into 1-inch pieces. Roll each piece in egg and place on baking sheet. Sprinkle with coarse salt. Bake 8 to 10 minutes or until golden brown. Brush with melted butter when done and sprinkle with a bit more salt. Delicious served warm and with mustard.

Columbus Oktoberfest

Columbus Oktoberfest

September

Ohio Expo Center / Ohio State Fairgrounds
717 East 17th Avenue • Columbus, OH 43211
614-444-5908 • www.columbusoktoberfest.com

Three 100 year old historic covered pavilions (100 thousand square feet) provide the perfect backdrop for two stages and dance floors for lots of polkas! The Columbus Oktoberfest is a huge celebration featuring races, children's activities, wine, music, shopping, games and of course, beer! For decades the Columbus Oktoberfest has been a mainstay in the Columbus area. It originated in Schiller Park, moved to the Ohio Expo Center, then set-up at multiple sites throughout German Village for several years. It has found its home back at the Ohio Expo Center and offers authentic-style facilities, the beautiful and spacious Natural Resources Park as well as paved parking and easy access to the event site. Come and celebrate Oktoberfest with the best beers and brats around.

Pretzel Bacon Appetizer

3 tablespoons maple syrup
1 pound bacon
1 (12-ounce) bag pretzel rods

Preheat oven to 350°. Brush maple syrup on 1 side of bacon. Wrap the side of bacon coated with maple syrup to inside of pretzel rod. Once bacon is wrapped around the pretzel rod, brush maple syrup on outside of bacon. Bake 15 minutes. Broil on high 1 minute. Turn pretzel rods and broil other side on high 1 minute to brown bacon.

Destination Hilliard

Beef Salami Log

2 pounds ground beef
1½ tablespoons Tender Quick salt
1½ tablespoons Worcestershire sauce
1 tablespoon liquid smoke
2 tablespoons fresh minced garlic
1½ tablespoons whole mustard seed
1 tablespoon pepper

Mix all ingredients well. Place in refrigerator overnight. Mix well again and form into 2 logs. Place on a metal rack on a cookie sheet. Place in 200° oven 8 to 10 hours, until logs appear dried through. Store in refrigerator or freezer. Serve with cheese and crackers.

Glass Rooster Cannery
Delaware County

Bacon Balsamic Deviled Eggs

12 eggs
4 slices bacon
½ cup mayonnaise
¼ cup minced red onion
2 teaspoons sugar
½ teaspoon balsamic vinegar
¼ teaspoon celery salt
¼ teaspoon freshly ground black pepper
¼ cup chopped fresh parsley

Place eggs in a large pot in a single layer and fill with water to cover by 1 inch. Cover saucepan and bring water to boil; immediately remove from heat and let eggs stand in hot water 15 minutes. Drain. Cool eggs under cold running water. Peel and halve lengthwise. Separate yolks from whites, placing yolks in a bowl; arrange egg whites with rounded side down onto a serving platter. Place bacon in a large, deep skillet and cook over medium-high heat, turning occasionally, until evenly browned, about 10 minutes. Drain on a paper towel-lined plate; chop. Mash yolks with a fork. Add bacon, mayonnaise, onion, sugar, balsamic vinegar, celery salt and pepper; stir until thoroughly combined. Spoon mixture into egg whites. Garnish with parsley.

Knox County Convention & Visitors Bureau

Basil and Bell Pepper Pesto

2 cups fresh basil leaves, packed
⅓ cup pine nuts
1 red bell pepper, seeded and chopped
3 garlic cloves, minced
½ cup grated Parmesan cheese
½ cup extra virgin olive oil
Salt and pepper to taste

Place basil leaves, pine nuts and bell pepper into food processor and pulse several times. Add garlic and Parmesan cheese and pulse several times more. Scrape down sides of food processor with a rubber spatula. While the food processor is running, slowly add olive oil in a steady thin stream. Occasionally stop to scrape down sides of food processor. Stir in salt and black pepper to taste. Delicious served with pasta or on crostini.

Vermilion Valley Vineyards

Kiwi and Pineapple Frushi

12 ounces coconut milk
½ cup water
½ cup jasmine rice
⅓ cup sugar
1 vanilla bean, halved and seeded
1 kiwi, peeled and quartered
1 pineapple, cored and cut into 4 (½x½x4-inch) rectangles
1½ cups sweetened coconut flakes, toasted*

Blend coconut milk, water, rice, sugar and vanilla bean in medium saucepan. Bring to boil over medium-high heat. Reduce heat to simmer, cover and cook 25 to 30 minutes, stirring frequently, until rice is tender and liquid is absorbed. Remove vanilla bean and drain off excess oil. Refrigerate until completely cooled.

Place a 20x10-inch piece of plastic wrap on work surface. Place cooled rice on plastic wrap and spread into 14x6-inch rectangle. Place kiwi quarters and pineapple pieces down center of rice making sure fruit pieces are touching. Using plastic wrap, start at long end of rice and roll into a 14-inch cylinder. Press 2 ends together tightly, completely surrounding fruit. Wrap tightly and refrigerate 2 or more hours. Remove plastic wrap and roll Frushi in toasted coconut, pressing to coat the rice. Trim Frushi ends, slice into ½-inch pieces. Garnish with fresh fruit or fruit purées.

Toasting coconut: Preheat oven to 350°. Spread coconut on baking pan. Bake 5 to 8 minutes or until toasted and golden brown. Shake pan as necessary to avoid burning.

Market Street Inn

Fresh Mint Tea

Tours at Ann's Raspberry Farm always include refreshing, fresh mint tea and samples of their Award-Winning Products. This perky tea is easy to make and always a favorite on a hot summer day.

6 sprigs fresh mint, each about 8 inches long
4 cups water
½ cup sugar

Wash mint sprigs well and twist stems a bit to release more of the mint flavor. Bring water to boil in saucepan. Put sprigs into boiling hot water and remove from heat. Let stand 15 minutes. Pour through strainer into a gallon pitcher. Add sugar. Fill pitcher with additional water and mix well. Fill a glass decanter with ice and pour tea over ice to serve.

Ann's Raspberry Farm

Some of Ann's Raspberry Farm's Award-Winning Products

Common Ground Canopy Tours Green Smoothie

1 cup orange juice
1 cup unsweetened almond milk
1 cup frozen pineapple
1 banana
½ cup frozen mango
½ cup organic kale
½ cup organic baby spinach
½ cup green organic chard
1 tablespoon unsweetened organic coconut flakes
10 ice cubes

Place ingredients, in order, in Vitamix or blender. Blend until smooth. Store leftover smoothie in air-tight container and save up to 24 hours.

Common Ground Canopy Tours

Common Ground Canopy Tours

14240 Baird Road • Oberlin, OH 44074
440-707-2044 • www.commongroundcenter.org

Common Ground Canopy Tours is nestled on 30-acres of a beautiful, wooded valley formed by the Vermilion River in Oberlin, Ohio. Participants experience breathtaking views while traversing between the tops of giant red and white oak, white pine, tulip poplar, and shaggy bark hickory trees.

The 2½-hour canopy tour consists of a 45-foot high tower, 7 zip lines, 13 tree platforms, 1 floating stairway, 3 sky bridges, and a rappel station providing a thrilling adventure and an incredible, uncommon view of the natural landscape. The peak height of the zipline is approximately 100 feet off the ground. Participants can soar through the sky at about 40 to 50 mph. Common Ground Canopy Tours boasts the only operational floating stairway in the entire country. Dynamic guides who act as storytellers, coaches, naturalists and technicians lead each tour.

Strawberry Wine Slush

½ pint fresh strawberries
⅔ cup Sauternes
½ (6-ounce) can frozen limeade concentrate
8 large ice cubes
Sugar, optional

In a blender container, combine fresh strawberries, Sauternes, frozen limeade concentrate and ice cubes. Blend until smooth. Add sugar if a sweeter flavor is desired. Serve immediately in stemmed glasses. Makes about 2½ cups slush.

Note: Slush may be transferred to a plastic container, covered, and frozen. Store in freezer for up to 4 weeks.

Troy Strawberry Festival

Troy Strawberry Festival

First weekend in June

405 SW Public Square, Suite 330 • Troy, OH
937-339-7714 • www.gostrawberries.com

In 1977, Troy held the first Strawberry Festival. Today more than 60 food booths offer everything from strawberry pizza, strawberry salsa, to strawberry kabobs, strawberry funnel cake, and strawberry cotton candy. There are even strawberry burritos! Whether the berry is short caked, chocolate dipped, blended, sliced, fried, or funnel caked, strawberries are the celebrated fruit. Best of all with each delicious bite the proceeds help raise funds for area non-profit organizations throughout the Miami Valley.

Over 260 artisans display and sell their quality-handcrafted items, including woodworking, metal crafts, jewelry, pottery, children's and pet items, glassware and much more. There are stages with free entertainment, a pie eating contest, car show, corn toss, 10K run and bike tour. The Strawberry Festival offers free parking and free shuttle service from various locations creating easy access to the festival location.

Summer Sangria

2 bottles semisweet white wine
12 ounces soda water
12 ounces ginger ale
1 whole orange, sliced thin crosswise
1 whole lemon, sliced thin crosswise
1 cup fresh sliced strawberries
1 cup fresh blueberries
Sprigs of mint

Combine wine, soda water, ginger ale, orange and lemon in a very large pitcher (or 2 small) and chill in refrigerator overnight.

An hour before serving, add strawberries and blueberries. Let chill for another hour and serve with sprigs of mint in tall glasses and long forks for eating the fruit. Great on a hot summer day!

Linda Basye, Piketon
Wine Tasting & Art Show

Wine Tasting & Art Show

Saturday before Thanksgiving • 12:00 to 4:00pm

Grand Restaurant & Tavern
104 East Emmitt Avenue • Waverly, OH 45690
740-947-9650 • www.piketravel.com

Each year the search for Ohio's award winning wines takes us from the Ohio River to the Lake Erie shore. The wines are paired with cheeses and luscious desserts along with regional artists' work in nine mediums which are judged and offered for sale that day. Live entertainment completes the setting for an enjoyable day that is both informative of the wide variety of Ohio wines available and also brings awareness of the arts. This event began in 1998 and continually attracts both the novice and the connoisseur of fine wine and fine art.

Polly Potter Kirtland's Cherry Bounce

8 cups fresh unpitted tart red cherries
2 cups sugar
1½ teaspoons whole allspice
1½ teaspoons whole cloves
2 inches stick cinnamon
4 cups bourbon

Wash and stem cherries. Place alternate layers of cherries, sugar and spices in a 2-quart jar. Pour in bourbon. Cover with cheesecloth. Stir daily until sugar is dissolved. Screw on top and place in cool, dark place for at least 2 months. Strain before serving in liqueur glasses. Makes 1 quart liqueur. This can make a second batch using the same cherries and spices. Strain aged liqueur into a decanter, then add more sugar and bourbon to the tart cherries and spices.

Mahoning Valley Historical Society

Mahoning Valley Historical Society
Operates

The Arms Family Museum
648 Wick Avenue
Youngstown, OH 44502

The Tyler Mahoning Valley History Center
325 West Federal Street
Youngstown, OH 44503
330-743-2589
www.mahoninghistory.org
Facebook, Twitter, Pinterest & Instagram: @mahoninghistory

Founded in 1875, The Mahoning Valley Historical Society (MVHS) celebrates the history of the Mahoning Valley, utilizing its significant collections of artifacts and archives. The Society operates The Arms Family Museum, located in a magnificent 1905 arts and crafts-period residence, and The Tyler Mahoning Valley History Center, a downtown Youngstown commercial building that was once the home of the Good Humor Ice Cream Bar. The Society serves over 20,000 people annually through interactive exhibits at both locations, outreach programs to schools, lectures, historic walking tours, and special community events. The Museum has been accredited by the American Association of Museums since 1977, a standard achieved by fewer than 10% of American museums.

Pumpkin Mule

A fall twist on a contemporary drink.

Juice of ½ lime
2 ounces Tito's vodka
4 to 6 ounces Rivertown Pumpkin Ale

Pour all into cocktail glass, over ice if preferred.

Dannie Devol
Old Man's Cave Chalets

Mulled Cider

½ gallon fresh-pressed apple cider
3 cinnamon sticks
2 whole cloves
2 allspice berries
1 thinly sliced orange

Place all ingredients in a large saucepan and bring to a simmer. Do not boil. Serve hot

Zoar School Inn Bed & Breakfast

Bread &
Breakfast

Buttermilk Cornbread

Vegetable oil cooking spray
1 cup white flour
1 cup yellow cornmeal
1 tablespoon baking powder
¼ teaspoon salt
¼ teaspoon baking soda
1¼ cups buttermilk
2 tablespoons sugar
1 egg
¼ cup vegetable oil
2 tablespoons butter

Preheat oven to 375°. Spray a 10-inch oven-ready skillet with oil and set aside. In a medium-size bowl, sift together flour, cornmeal, baking powder and salt. In a separate bowl, combine baking soda and buttermilk. Whisk in sugar, egg and vegetable oil. Heat prepared skillet over medium heat, add butter and heat until it just starts to sizzle. Add wet mixture to dry mixture and stir quickly. Scrape batter into prepared pan and bake until golden brown, about 20 minutes. Let cool and slice into wedges to serve.

BIG BEND BLUES BASH

Big Bend Blues Bash

Last full weekend in July

Downtown Pomeroy, OH 45769
800-MEIGS-CO • www.pomeroyblues.org

The blues is a genre of music celebrated year after year at the Pomeroy Big Bend Blues Bash. This weekend-long festival features some of the biggest names in blues, celebrating a variety of styles from acoustic to electric. There are kids' activities, delicious food, and other forms of entertainment suitable for every taste. All of this happens along the banks of the majestic Ohio River. The Bash is a summer favorite and not to be missed. Grab some friends, grabs some chairs, sit back and relax to the blues as it's meant to be heard.

Apricot White Chocolate Bread

1 cup snipped dried apricots
2 cups warm water
1 cup sugar
2 tablespoons butter, softened
1 egg
¾ cup orange juice
Orange zest from orange
2 cups flour
2 teaspoons baking powder
¼ teaspoon baking soda
1 teaspoon salt
¼ to ½ cup white chocolate chunks
¾ cup chopped pecans or macadamia nuts

Soak apricots in warm water for 30 minutes. Meanwhile, in a bowl, cream together sugar, butter and egg. Stir in orange juice and zest. In separate bowl, combine flour, baking powder, baking soda and salt; stir into creamed mixture until combined. Drain apricots well; add to batter; add white chocolate chunks and nuts. Pour into a greased 9x5-inch loaf pan. Bake at 350° for 55 minutes or until bread tests done. Cool 10 minutes in pan before removing to a wire rack.

Zoar School Inn Bed & Breakfast

Zoar School Inn Bed & Breakfast

160 East Third Street, Box 509 • Zoar, OH 44697
216-927-3700 • www.zoarschoolinn.com

The Zoar School Inn Bed & Breakfast was Zoar's first schoolhouse built in 1836. The structure was turned into a residence when a new school was built. Four private bedrooms with bath have been decorated for the ultimate in sheer pleasure and comfort. Guests will step back in time to enjoy charm of the historic village of Zoar. Furnished and decorated with old world style in mind, private bedroom suites are designed as a 'home away from home'. Call or visit their website for additional information or to make reservations.

Amish Granola Bread

Voted Favorite Bread by B&B guests.

1⅔ cups water
⅓ cup honey
2 tablespoons butter
1 teaspoon salt
3½ cups high-gluten flour
1 cup rolled oats
2 teaspoons bread machine yeast
1 cup Amish granola (we like Country Lane Granola from Walnut Creek Cheese)
¾ cup golden raisins

Put ingredients in bread machine pan in the order listed. Set bread machine for a 2-pound loaf of sweet bread and bake.

Note: If dough seems dry when it starts mixing, add 2 teaspoons of water as needed. This recipe is for a bread machine but could be adapted to baking in a regular oven.

Garden Gate Get-A-Way

Garden Gate Get-A-Way Bed & Breakfast

6041 Township Road 310 • Millersburg, OH 44654
330-674-7608 • www.garden-gate.com

This award-winning bed and breakfast is located in Holmes County, Ohio. Not only is this area home to the World's Largest Amish Community but it hosts everything that tourists like to do. There are wineries, breweries, cheese factories, chocolate factory, dining, shopping, golf, nature trails, antiques, museums and more. At the end of each day guests are pampered at the bed and breakfast with special features in the room, flower gardens to relax in, plus an evening campfire to unwind. The home cooked breakfasts are the "icing on the cake." The B&B owns a tour bus and offers a variety of itineraries. Guests can even have dinner with an Amish neighbor.

Pumpkin Bread

Makes two loaves.

2 cups sugar
1 cup oil
4 eggs
½ cup water
3½ cups flour
4 teaspoons cinnamon
2 teaspoons baking soda
1 teaspoon salt
½ teaspoon ground cloves
2 cups canned pumpkin
1 cup chopped pecans
½ cup raisins

Combine sugar and oil, beat in eggs 1 at a time. Mix in water. In a separate bowl, combine flour, cinnamon, baking soda, salt and cloves. Stir in egg mixture. Stir in pumpkin. Add nuts and raisins last. Pour into 2 (9x13-inch) greased loaf pans. Bake about 1 hour at 350°. Cool 10 minutes and turn out onto racks to cool completely. Can be frozen up to 1 month.

Circleville Pumpkin Show

Circleville Pumpkin Show

Third Wednesday in October

159 East Franklin Street • Circleville, OH 43113
740-474-7000

The Circleville Pumpkin Show attracts over 400,000 visitors to the small Midwest community of just over 13,000 people. Visitors from all 50 states and many foreign counties come to see the giant pumpkins, parades, entertainment, contests, and sample all the pumpkin flavored delicacies. Each year the Circleville Pumpkin Show kicks off with area pumpkin growers vying for the coveted Giant Pumpkin Champion Trophy and cash prize for first place. There is live music, seven parades each with a different theme, fantastic amusement rides, and over 400 food booths, games and craft vendors. Most of the foods at the Circleville Pumpkin Show are pumpkin-related: pumpkin pies, donuts, cookies, burgers, pizza, tacos, chili, elephant ears, pancakes, taffy, ice cream, cake, waffles, cream puffs, fudge, brownies and many other pumpkin treats. Come and experience "The Greatest Free Show on Earth!"

Pumpkin Muffins

2 cups pumpkin purée
1 cup packed brown sugar
¼ cup oil
¼ cup unsweetened applesauce
½ cup water
4 eggs
2 teaspoons vanilla
1 cup white flour
1 cup whole-wheat flour
1 cup rolled oats
4 teaspoons baking powder
2 teaspoons pumpkin pie spice
¼ teaspoon nutmeg
1 teaspoon salt
1 cup chopped nuts
1 cup dark chocolate chips

Preheat oven to 375° and spray muffin cups with nonstick spray or line with paper muffin cups. Combine pumpkin purée, sugar, oil, applesauce, water, eggs and vanilla. Stir or whisk until smooth.

Add flours, oats, baking powder and spices. Stir just until moistened. Add nuts and chocolate chips and stir just until mixed in. Do not over mix—this makes tough muffins. Bake 20 minutes or until edges are lightly browned and a toothpick inserted into a muffin comes out clean. Cool on a clean tea towel or cooling rack.

Holly Larson, Grass Roots Nutrition
Oxford Visitors Bureau

Oxford Farmers Market

East Park Place • Oxford, OH 45056
www.oxfordfarmersmarket.com

Saturdays: Weekly, May-November and monthly December-April.

Held in historic Uptown Oxford, this Farmers Market is more than just produce. This award winning market features chocolatiers, artisans, coffee, little sprout children's activities, live music and cooking demonstrations.

Apple Butter Pecan Muffins

1 large apple, sliced thin and chopped (1½ cups)
½ teaspoon cinnamon
½ cup plus 1 tablespoon sugar
½ cup butter, softened
1 cup apple butter
2 eggs
2 cups flour
1 tablespoon baking powder
1 cup coarsely chopped pecans

Preheat oven to 375°. In a medium bowl, toss chopped apple with cinnamon and 1 tablespoon sugar to coat thoroughly. Set aside. In mixing bowl, cream butter, apple butter and ½ cup sugar until well blended, about 4 minutes. Add eggs and mix well. In a medium bowl, blend flour and baking powder. Add to creamed mixture, blending well. Stir in chopped apples and pecans. Spoon into greased or paper-lined muffin tins. Bake 15 to 20 minutes. Makes 18.

Grand Rapids Applebutter Fest

Grand Rapids Applebutter Fest

Second Sunday in October

Grand Rapids, OH 43522
www.applebutterfest.org
www.facebook.com/grapplebutterfest

Since 1977, the Historical Society of Grand Rapids has organized the Applebutter Fest, with something for everyone in the family! Walk along the canal path and see Civil War and WWII encampment and talk with the interpreters. Participate in pioneer crafts, listen to live music on several stages throughout the Fest, and visit the children's entertainment area with jugglers, magicians, and storytellers. There are classic cars, antique farm equipment, farm life demonstrations, handmade juried crafts with a wide range of collectibles and gifts, many varieties of fabulous food, and (of course) homemade apple butter made on site in copper kettles over an open fire. Admission is free, complimentary shuttle service with parking $10. Visit the website for yearly event information and detailed driving directions.

Raisin Bran Muffins

6 to 8 cups Raisin Bran cereal
3 cups sugar
5 cups flour
5 teaspoons baking soda
3 teaspoons salt
1 teaspoon cloves
1 teaspoon nutmeg
1 teaspoon cinnamon
4 beaten eggs
1 cup oil
2 teaspoons vanilla
1 quart buttermilk
1 cup chopped walnuts

Preheat oven to 400°. Combine cereal, sugar, flour, baking soda, salt, cloves, nutmeg and cinnamon; mix well. In a separate bowl, combine eggs, oil, vanilla and buttermilk. Add egg mixture to flour mixture. Mix well. Fold in walnuts. Fill greased muffin tins two thirds or more full. Bake 20 minutes.

Zanesville-Muskingum County Convention and Visitors Bureau

Zanesville-Muskingum County Convention and Visitors Bureau

205 North Fifth Street • Zanesville, OH 43701
800-743-2303 • www.visitzanesville.com

Zanesville-Muskingum County has fun for the whole family! Visitors and locals alike can partake in many different adventures. Take a safari tour at the Wilds and a Lorena Sternwheeler cruise on the Muskingum River. To fire the creative side, experience the Artist Colony of Zanesville and First Friday Art Walk. Be sure to tour the John and Annie Glenn Historic Site, National Road-Zane Grey Museum, Dr. Increase Mathews House Museum, Stone Academy, Zanesville Museum of Art and more. When it's time to sit back and relax, pay a visit to Weasel Boy Brewing Co. and local wineries. There are state parks, beautiful gardens, the Village of Dresden, Longaberger Homestead, antique shops, specialty stores and pottery outlets. For the outdoorsman and athletically inclined, enjoy golfing, biking, hunting, fishing and boating. Sample local cuisine then get a comfortable night's rest at one of the hotels, inns, B & B's, cabins or campgrounds.

Fall Harvest Muffins

2 cups peeled shredded apples
1⅓ cups sugar
1 cup chopped cranberries
1 cup shredded carrots
2 eggs, beaten
½ cup canola oil
2½ cups flour
1 tablespoon baking powder
2 teaspoons baking soda
1 tablespoon ground cinnamon
½ teaspoon salt

Preheat oven to 375° and line muffin pan with paper liners. Combine apples and sugar in a bowl and let stand 5 to 10 minutes. Add cranberries, carrots, eggs and canola oil; mix well. In a separate bowl combine flour, baking powder, baking soda, cinnamon and salt. Combine wet and dry mixtures until just moistened. Fill muffin cups three-quarters full. Bake 25 to 30 minutes or until a toothpick inserted comes out clean.

Garden Gate Get-A-Way

Giant Cinnamon Rolls

4 tablespoons melted butter
4 tablespoons water
½ (3.4-ounce) box instant vanilla pudding
1 cup milk
1 egg
1 tablespoon sugar
½ teaspoon salt
4 cups bread flour
2½ teaspoons yeast

Place ingredients in bread machine following specifications for that particular machine. Set for dough cycle. After dough cycle is complete, remove from machine and roll out to a rectangle approximately 17x10 inches.

Filling:

1 cup brown sugar
2 teaspoons cinnamon
½ cup softened butter

Mix together brown sugar and cinnamon. Spread softened butter over dough. Sprinkle brown sugar and cinnamon mixture over top. Roll tightly from long end, pinching edges closed when completely rolled. Slice rolled dough into ¾-inch slices. Place into greased cake pans (usually get 15 buns). Let rise until doubled. Bake at 350° for 15 to 20 minutes, until golden. Do not overbake.

Frosting:

4 ounces softened cream cheese
¼ cup butter
1½ cups powdered sugar
½ teaspoon vanilla
1½ teaspoons milk

Mix ingredients together until well blended and spread over very warm rolls. They are best when eaten fresh.

Fitzgerald's Irish Bed & Breakfast

Sausage and Egg Muffins

¾ cup flour
1½ teaspoons baking powder
¼ teaspoon salt
1 teaspoon butter
1 pound turkey sausage, cooked
6 eggs
½ to 1 cup Cheddar cheese, shredded

Combine all ingredients; mix well. Scoop into greased muffin tins, fill three-quarters full. Bake 20 minutes at 350°.

Sue Whitaker, Fair Secretary
Fulton County Fair

Fulton County Fair

8514 State Route 108 • Wauseon, OH 43567
419-335-6006 • www.fultoncountyfair.com

The Fulton County Fair, founded in 1858, is conveniently located at exit 34 of the Ohio Turnpike in the rural town of Wauseon, Ohio. As the urban sprawl has encroached on many county fairs, the Fulton County Fair has, with the support of its dedicated community, kept its mission of providing a family-friendly event that promotes its agricultural heritage. The Fulton County Fair has an attendance of over 280,000 fairgoers, making it one of the top three fairs in the state of Ohio. The Fair fills nearly 30 barns and tents with a variety of animals, fine arts, antiques, culinary, and agricultural exhibits plus local merchants. And, one can't fail to mention the over 100 food vendors that serve up an unprecedented variety of mouth-watering "Fair Food". Entertainment abounds at the Fair, from Jr. Fair judging to top-name country acts and everything in between.

Whole Grain Pancakes

½ cup all-purpose flour
¼ cup oat flour
¼ cup whole-wheat flour
¼ cup spelt flour
¼ cup almond flour
¼ cup coconut flour
½ teaspoon baking soda
½ teaspoon salt
¼ cup ground flax seeds
⅛ cup poppy seeds
¼ cup chopped pecans
2 beaten eggs
¼ cup melted butter
1 cup buttermilk

Combine flours, baking soda and salt together. Add seeds and nuts and stir to combine. Add eggs, melted butter and buttermilk and mix well. Pour ¼ cup batter onto heated griddle. Flip when tiny bubbles appear on surface, cook for about 40 seconds. Serve warm with favorite syrup or honey.

Asian Festival

May

Franklin Park

1755 East Broad Street • Columbus, OH 43203

www.asian-festival.org

This annual event with more than 100,000 visitors continues to grow thanks to the strong participation of many people regardless of origin and ethnicity. Recognized as one of the most important, the Asian Festival has a wide variety of activities and entertainment throughout the weekend. The Gala, wonderful Asian food, games, a career fair, children's activities, cultural exhibits, dragon boat races, a health pavilion, a terrific market place, martial arts demonstrations and other performances ensure this festival to be one of the premier events in Columbus, year after year.

After the Morning Flight Breakfast

Set up the night before in a large slow cooker and take out in the morning and turn on high before you leave to fly. Breakfast will be ready when you get home. Just make coffee and pour the juice!

1 (16-ounce) bag frozen shredded hash browns
1 pound diced ham
1 red pepper, diced
1 medium onion, diced
3 cups shredded Cheddar cheese
1 dozen eggs
1 cup milk
Salt and pepper

In slow cooker make 3 equal layers of potatoes, ham, pepper, onion, cheese. Beat eggs with milk and slowly pour over layered ingredients. Salt and pepper as desired. Cook 4 hours on high. Can add other vegetables, varieties of cheese or use bacon or sausage.

Feeds a hungry hot air balloon pilot, the crew and a guest or two.

Ashland Balloonfest

Ashland Balloonfest

July

Freer Field

1256 Center Street • Ashland, OH 44805

www.ashlandohioballoonfest.com

Ashland Balloonfest promises to be an outing with the entire family in mind. Celebrating 25 years in 2015, everyone enjoys the colorful skies as the hot air balloons fill the air for a memorable weekend near the 4th of July holiday. Delight in the festivities! Each year will have a new experience to treasure for years to come. Entertainment, music, shows, and an assortment of food vending is all part of the nonstop activities. Ashland, Ohio is an easy hour or so drive on 1-71 South of Cleveland, north of Columbus. Visit their website or like them on Facebook for up-to-date information.

The Inn's Signature Smoked Salmon Seven-Cheese Frittata

Canola oil spray
3 tablespoons butter, divided
1 pound small new red potatoes, washed, cut in eighths
½ ounce fresh rosemary, chopped
1 teaspoon Beau Monde seasoning
½ teaspoon white pepper
1 Vidalia onion, sliced and halved
1 leek, sliced
1 red bell pepper, sliced into strips and halved
1 tablespoon sugar
1 (14-ounce) can artichoke hearts
4 ounces fresh spinach
8 ounces smoked salmon, sliced into small pieces
12 to 14 fresh eggs
2 ounces provolone cheese, shredded
2 ounces mozzarella cheese, shredded
2 ounces white Cheddar cheese, shredded
2 ounces Asiago cheese, shredded
4 ounces goat cheese, crumbled
4 fresh Roma tomatoes, sliced
6 to 8 ounces Parmesan cheese, shredded
3 ounces Gruyère cheese, shredded

Preheat oven to 325° on broil. Grease sauté pan with canola oil. Add 2 tablespoons butter. Add potatoes, rosemary, Beau Monde seasoning, and white pepper. Sauté 30 minutes on medium heat, covered, stirring regularly. In separate greased pan, sauté onion, leek and bell pepper with remaining 1 tablespoon butter. Sprinkle sugar over mixture to help caramelize. Sauté 20 minutes on low heat, increasing heat slightly last 2 to 3 minutes. Combine sautéed vegetables, artichoke hearts, spinach and smoked salmon into 1 pan. In separate bowl, beat eggs well. Add provolone, mozzarella, Cheddar and Asiago cheeses to egg mixture; stir well. Add half egg mixture to vegetables. Cook on low heat, with lid, until it begins to firm. Add goat cheese and remaining egg mixture to pan. Continue cooking, with lid, 5 to 7 minutes. Top with tomatoes followed by Parmesan and Gruyère cheeses. Broil on middle rack of oven 7 to 8 minutes. Cool 10 minutes. Slice into wedges and serve.

The Welsh Hills Inn

The Welsh Hills Inn

A Country Bed & Breakfast

2133 Cambria Mill Road • Granville, OH 43023
740-321-1493 • www.WelshHillsInn.com
Reservations: www.BookTheInn.com
Availability Calendar: www.InnAvailability.com
Gift Certificates: www.InnGiftCertificate.com
Facebook: www.facebook.com/GranvillesInn
Twitter: www.twitter.com/WelshHillsInn

Ohio's premier bed & breakfast lodging nestled on 15 wooded acres in the beautiful Welsh Hill's equestrian and alpaca countryside. Wide plank heart pine floors, four large guest rooms (including a suite), luxurious bedding, and spacious bathrooms highlight The Inn in the picturesque, New England-like Village of Granville. The walls and halls are adorned with antiques and original artwork. Enjoy the outdoor heated pool and gardens, explore the hiking trails, stocked pond, bocce ball court, shooting ranges, plus darts and outdoor table tennis. Guests enjoy a complimentary, Signature home-cooked breakfast each morning—plus wine, cheese, and light refreshments daily. Relax by a roaring fire at the outdoor fireplace or in The Inn's state-of-the-art hot tub nestled by the forest. Relax to a simpler time with all of today's modern conveniences.

- **TripAdvisor Travelers' Choice Award:**
  Rated #1 B&B and Inn in the United States
  Rated in the Top 5 B&Bs and Inns in the World
- **B&B/Inn of the Year—Ohio Hotel & Lodging Association**

Holiday Baked Egg

3 strips bacon per serving
1 (16-ounce) package phyllo dough
2 tablespoons shredded Swiss cheese per serving
1 egg per serving
Pinch of garlic powder
Salt and pepper to taste
2 tablespoons medium salsa per serving
2 tablespoons shredded Cheddar cheese per serving
Mushrooms, sliced and sautéed, optional

Spray cooking spray into 4½x½-inch round tart pans per serving. Microwave bacon to medium well; cool and cut into 1-inch-wide strips. Cut phyllo dough into 5-inch squares. Place 3 thin squares of phyllo dough into each pan. Place 4 to 5 (1-inch) pieces of prepared bacon inside the rim of each tart pan, then place Swiss cheese inside the tart and push the cheese toward the edge. This will create a "nest" for the egg so it stays centered. (Often the egg yolk bumps against a piece of fried bacon, and the sharp edge will break the yolk. This little "nest" works to avoid yolk breakage.) Sprinkle garlic, salt and pepper onto egg; place salsa on 1 side of the pan and garnish with Cheddar cheese and mushrooms. Bake at 350° for about 35 minutes. When serving you may eat in pan or slip onto plate. This is cute baked in any individual-size serving dish.

The Barn Inn Bed and Breakfast

The Barn Inn Bed and Breakfast

6838 County Road 203 • Millersburg, OH 44654
330-674-7600 • www.thebarninn.com

The Barn Inn Bed and Breakfast, a restored barn in Ohio's Amish Country, serves as the perfect retreat, a place to refresh and enjoy all things authentic. The Inn, located only two hours from Cleveland and Columbus, is located in Holmes County, a region where people have maintained their distinct European origins and where food, art, and work reflect the hearts and hands of the people. Horse and carriage travel is the norm, harvest fields, like patchwork, adorn the countryside and artisan crafts and authentic foods abound.

Luxury suites feature exterior and interior hallway entrances, privacy, cozy fireplaces, and en suite baths with Jacuzzis. Amenities include wifi, evening pastries, TV, DVD, A/C, and an exceptional country breakfast daily, followed by an area informational. In-room massages, wine and cheese baskets, Amish tours and meal packages are available. Picturesque grounds with fountains, bridge over Honey Run Creek, and wooded park offer rest and relaxation.

Bacon and Egg Lasagna

1 pound bacon, cut in 1-inch strips
1 cup chopped onions
⅓ cup bacon drippings
⅓ cup flour
½ teaspoon salt
¼ teaspoon pepper
4 cups milk
12 lasagna noodles, cooked and drained
12 hard-cooked eggs, sliced
2 cups (8 ounces) shredded Swiss cheese
⅓ cup grated Parmesan cheese
2 tablespoons chopped parsley

In large skillet, cook bacon until crisp; drain, reserving ⅓ cup drippings. Set bacon aside. Cook onions in bacon drippings until tender. Add flour, salt and pepper; stir until paste forms. Add milk; cook and stir until mixture comes to a boil and is thickened. Heat oven to 350°. Grease 9x13-inch baking dish. Spoon a small amount of white sauce into bottom of pan. Divide lasagna noodles, bacon, white sauce, eggs and Swiss cheese into thirds; layer in pan. Sprinkle with Parmesan cheese. Bake 25 to 30 minutes or until thoroughly heated. Sprinkle with parsley. Let stand 10 minutes before serving. Makes 12 servings.

Make Ahead Tip: Assemble the day before. Cover and refrigerate. Bake, covered, at 350° for 25 minutes. Remove cover, bake 15 to 20 minutes longer or until hot.

Fitzgerald's Irish Bed & Breakfast

Fitzgerald's Irish Bed & Breakfast

47 Mentor Avenue • Painesville, OH 44077
www.FitzgeraldBB.com

Nestled in the heart of Painesville is a remarkable French Tudor, Fitzgerald's Irish Bed & Breakfast. This beautifully restored sixteen-room home is a destination in and of itself, with unique details throughout. Each guest room summons the imagery of various Irish locations such as Galway and Dublin, giving visitors a cozy resting place that is a vacation within a vacation. There are special touches throughout the home that add a special touch to each guests stay; delicate Irish teacups, treats tucked away for quick snacks, warm and delicious breakfast, and amenities available to suit different needs. Fitzgerald's Irish Bed & Breakfast is located just 30 miles from downtown Cleveland. The area offers over 35 wineries, Lake Erie beaches, museums, restaurants and shopping. Visit their website for rates and reservations for an Irish experience in the great state of Ohio.

Gluten-Free Scotch Eggs with Cheddar Cheese Sauce

Eggs:

10 eggs, divided
16 sausage patties
3 cups finely crushed gluten-free cornflakes
1½ cups cornstarch
2 tablespoons water
½ cup vegetable oil

Preheat oven to 350°. Hard-boil 8 eggs and peel when cool. Place sausage patties on parchment paper and slightly flatten with your hand or spatula. Place cornflake crumbs in a bowl. Place 1½ cups cornstarch in a separate shallow bowl and make an egg wash in a third bowl by beating 2 remaining eggs with water. Dredge boiled eggs in cornstarch then wrap each egg in 2 sausage patties; pinch patty edges together to seal. Roll each egg in your hands (like a meatball) to ensure sausage covers egg, then set aside. (At this point eggs may be covered and refrigerated overnight.) Dredge each sausage-covered egg in cornstarch, then in egg wash and finally in cornflake crumbs until well coated. Using 1 large or 2 small oven-safe frying pans, heat oil to 350° (small amount of cornstarch dropped in pan will sizzle). Add eggs to pan and bake 30 minutes, turning every 7 to 8 minutes.

Cheese Sauce:

4 tablespoons butter
4 tablespoons cornstarch
2 cups milk
½ teaspoon salt
¼ teaspoon pepper
1½ cups finely shredded Cheddar cheese, divided
¼ cup chopped parsley

(CONTINUED)

Cheese Sauce:

Melt butter in saucepan. Remove from burner and rapidly whisk in cornstarch. Return to burner and add milk, stirring to incorporate butter mixture. Continue to stir until sauce has thickened, approximately 5 minutes. Add salt, pepper and 1 cup shredded cheese and stir until cheese is melted. Add more milk to thin, if needed.

Remove eggs from pan and let rest on cutting board 5 to 6 minutes. Carefully slice each egg in half, placing both halves on a plate, egg side up. Drizzle with cheese sauce and garnish with remaining cheese and parsley.

Homestead House Bed & Breakfast

Connie Beverage, Events Coordinator, Homestead House Bed & Breakfast

Market Street Inn Granola

5 cups rolled oats
1 cup blanched slivered almonds
1 cup chopped walnuts
1 cup chopped pecans
1 cup sesame seeds
1 cup wheat germ
2 cups shredded coconut
1 cup unsalted sunflower seeds
1 cup canola oil
1½ cups honey
2 cups dried fruit (raisins, cranberries, dates, etc.)

Preheat oven to 325°. In a large bowl, stir together oats, almonds, walnuts, pecans, sesame seeds, wheat germ, coconut and sunflower seeds. In a small pan over medium heat, stir together oil and honey. Cook and stir until blended. Pour over oat mixture and stir to coat evenly. Spread out in an even layer on 2 cookie sheets. Bake 20 minutes until the oats and nuts are toasted. Stir after first 10 minutes and rotate cookie sheets in oven. Immediately after it comes out of oven, stir in dried fruit. Let stand until cooled and stir again to break up any large clusters. Store in an airtight container.

Market Street Inn

Market Street Inn

356 North Market Street
Wooster, OH 44691
330-262-4085
www.marketstreetinnwooster.com

Located in historic downtown Wooster, Ohio, Market Street Inn is an elegant 1897 Victorian mansion. The three-story home with its welcoming front porch and majestic red turret, features stunning original woodwork, parquet floors, spectacular period stained-glass windows, and restored embossed ceilings. The Inn has five guest rooms all with private baths, and two with antique claw foot tubs.

The Inn is walking distance from The College of Wooster, The Ohio Light Opera theatre, and Wooster's exceptional downtown restaurants and boutiques. America's largest Amish community is only a twenty-five minute country drive south of the Inn.

Food takes center stage at Market Street Inn, where a full service breakfast including the house specialty scones, and gourmet starters and entrees are prepared using the bounty of local produce and the Inn's own vegetable and herb garden.

Strawberry-Pineapple Jam

2 cups strawberries, crushed
3 cups pineapple (fresh or frozen), crushed
1 teaspoon butter
⅓ cup powdered pectin
6½ cups sugar

Combine strawberries, pineapple, butter and pectin in pot. Bring to rolling boil. Add sugar all at once. Bring back to rolling boil for 2 or 3 minutes, until liquid slowly drips off spoon like thick honey. Place in canning jars leaving ¼-inch headspace. Wipe rims, put seals and rings on jars. Place in large pot of hot water, covering jars by at least 1 inch. Bring to boil and process 5 minutes. Remove from boiling water and let rest on counter until cool. Check each jar for a good seal by pressing on the lid before placing it on your shelf. (If lid pops back, it didn't seal. Store the jar in your refrigerator.)

Glass Rooster Cannery
Delaware County

The Glass Rooster Cannery is the only cannery of its type in Ohio. Take a class in canning, dehydrating, fermenting, or cheese making, or plan a private cooking event with family or friends.

1673 South State Route 605 • Sunbury, Ohio 43074 • 614-499-2958 • glassroostercannery.com

Delaware County

34 South Sandusky Street • Delaware, OH 43015

Delaware County offers big-time attractions and small-town charm right in the center of Ohio. Visitors enjoy arts, culture, events and local history in charming Midwest towns that sprouted up in the 1800's. The Columbus Zoo and Aquarium, Zoombezi Bay, Olentangy Indian Caverns, two State Parks and 11 Preservation Parks provide endless outdoor fun. Four inland lakes offer lots of water recreation.

Whether you have a taste for hometown and homemade or chef-created culinary delights, there are many places to dine in Delaware County. Local breweries, wineries, and farmer's markets tastefully compliment the local cuisine. Dine at the historic Bun's restaurant or Hamburger Inn—the two oldest restaurants in the County (see recipes). Many new and trendy eating establishments are also located throughout the area, featuring American, Asian, Greek, Italian, Mexican, Cajun, and other yummy foods.

For more information about things to do and places to stay, check out www.visitdeloho.com, call 1-888-DEL-OHIO (335-6446), or find us on Facebook, Twitter, and Instagram.

Jalapeño Jelly

6 cups sugar
2 cups cider vinegar
8 large jalapeño peppers, chopped
2 (3-ounce) pouches liquid pectin

Bring sugar and vinegar to boil. Add peppers; bring back to a boil. Add pectin and bring back to a boil. Pour into jars, let cool. Enjoy!

Recipe courtesy of Baumbach's Pit Bar-B-Que
617 South Washington Street, New Paris, Ohio
937-437-8151
Preble County Convention & Visitors Bureau

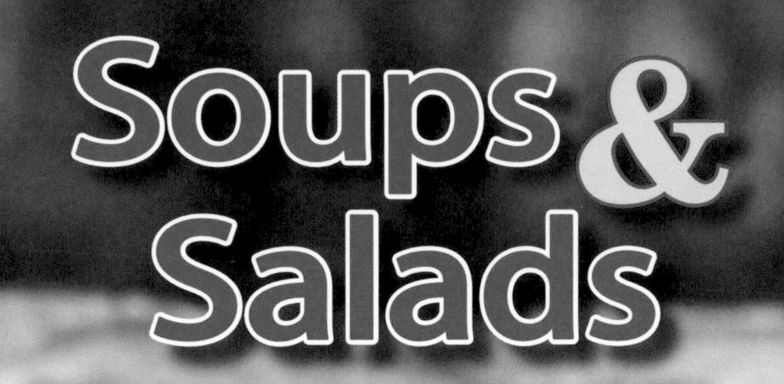
Soups &
Salads

Kartoffel Suppe

(Potato Soup)

2 cups raw potatoes, cubed
1 small onion, finely chopped
1 quart water
1 quart milk
1½ cups noodles
½ teaspoon nutmeg
1 teaspoon salt
3 tablespoons butter
1 cup small bread cubes

Cook the potatoes and onion in 1 quart water until tender. Add 1 quart milk and bring to a boil. Add noodles, nutmeg and salt. Cook slowly until noodles are tender. In skillet, put butter and bread cubes. Fry until golden brown. Add to soup and serve.

Historic Zoar Village

ZOAR COMMUNITY ASSOCIATION

Historic Zoar Village

198 Main Street
Zoar, OH 44697
330-874-3011 • 800-262-6195
www.historiczoarvillage.com
Facebook: Zoar Community Association
Twitter: ZoarOhio

APRIL, MAY, AND OCTOBER:
Saturday 11am to 4pm
Sunday 12pm to 4pm

JUNE THROUGH SEPTEMBER:
Wednesday through Saturday 11am to 4pm
Sunday 12pm to 4pm

Other days and times by appointment

ANDY DONALDSON, HISTORIC ZOAR VILLAGE

Zoar Village was founded in 1817 by a group of 200 German Separatists seeking escape from religious persecution in their homeland. After a difficult start, the immigrants decided to cast their lots together and form a communal society. These Separatists thrived as a unique Society for more than 80 years, making Zoar Village one of the most successful communal settlements in American history. The food of Zoar included nearly all the recipes considered today as traditional German recipes. Dried apples, or snitz, sauerkraut and veal schnitzel were often served. The women made spaetzle and noodles, and were served in communal kitchens. Today, Zoar Village is made up of approximately 75 families living in homes built from 1817 to the present. Come and tour the museums, see early American architecture and enjoy the quaint village scenery.

Erbsensuppe

(Pea Soup)

¼ cup bacon, diced
½ cup chopped onion
1 carrot, chopped
1 celery stalk, chopped
1 pound dried peas
8 cups chicken stock
2 cups half-and-half
1 clove garlic
1 teaspoon ground coriander
3 sprigs fresh thyme

In a small stockpot, sauté bacon until lightly crisp. Add onion, carrot and celery; sauté until tender. Add dried peas, chicken stock, half-and-half, garlic, coriander and thyme. Simmer 1 hour until peas are tender and pasty. Purée until smooth with a blender. Salt and pepper to taste.

Canal Tavern of Zoar

Canal Tavern of Zoar

8806 Towpath Road NE • Bolivar, OH 44612
Located just outside Historic Zoar Village
330-874-4444 • www.canaltavernofzoar.com

Wednesday through Sunday
Lunch 11:30am to 2pm
Dinner 4:30pm to 9pm (weekdays) and 4:30pm to 10pm (weekends)

The Canal Tavern of Zoar is a fine casual restaurant in an 1829 Ohio and Erie Canal tavern located just outside Historic Zoar Village on the Towpath Trail. The terrific menu includes German dishes with Zoar connection as well as steaks, chops and seafood. A large selection of fine wines and craft beers is available. There is outside dining on the patio in season and private dining rooms for six to fifty.

Italian Sausage & Cabbage Soup

1 pound mild Italian sausage, cut into 1-inch cubes
1 (10.75-ounce) can tomato soup
1 soup can water
2 cups coarsely chopped cabbage
1 package frozen Italian green beans
½ teaspoon Italian seasoning
¼ teaspoon garlic powder
½ cup uncooked elbow macaroni

Brown sausage in large pot. Add remaining ingredients and bring to a boil. Lower temperature and simmer 45 to 60 minutes. Serve hot and garnish with shredded mozzarella, if desired.

Cheryl McIntosh
Parma Area Chamber of Commerce

Parma, OH 44129

www.parmaareachamber.org
440-886-1700

The Parma Area Chamber of Commerce and the Council of Smaller Enterprises (COSE) have formed an alliance that benefit area businesses. Through a special joint membership agreement, businesses in Parma, Parma Heights and Seven Hills and the surrounding communities can now join both organizations and save $150 or more on what it would have cost to join each of them separately. As a result of this unique partnership, area businesses get valuable exposure and resources in their local communities.

Puréed Cauliflower Soup

4 ounces (1 stick) unsalted butter
2 heads fresh cauliflower, roughly chopped (can use frozen if fresh is unavailable)
1 medium Spanish onion, sliced
2 carrots, peeled and chopped
3 stalks celery, chopped
1 shallot, minced
2 cups dry white wine
2 Idaho potatoes, peeled and chopped
½ gallon milk
1 pint cream
2 bay leaves
Kosher salt and pepper
3 sprigs thyme
5 sprigs rosemary

In a large pot heat butter until bubbling and add cauliflower; cook until golden brown. Add onion, carrots, celery and shallot and sweat veggies. Add wine and deglaze pan, making sure the wine boils to prevent splitting the dairy. Add potatoes, milk, cream, bay leaves, 1 tablespoon salt and 1 teaspoon pepper and water to cover. Tie thyme and rosemary in a bouquet and add to the pot. Simmer 30 minutes until potatoes are tender. Remove from heat and cool; remove herb bouquet and bay leaves. Purée mixture carefully. Taste and adjust seasoning.

The Galley
203 Second Street • Marietta, OH 45750
740-374-8278

Brussels Sprout Soup

1 rutabaga, peeled and cubed
1 small butternut squash, peeled and cubed
1 extra large onion, chopped
3 small potatoes, peeled and cubed
3 cloves garlic, minced
1 celery stalk, sliced
2 pounds whole Brussels sprouts, trimmed
1 (48-ounce) can chicken broth
1 large bay leaf
8 Italian sausage links (casing removed), browned and sliced
Salt and pepper to taste

Put all vegetables, chicken broth and bay leaf in a large soup pot. Place sausage on top. (It will finish cooking with the vegetables.) Place on medium heat and cover. Add salt and pepper. Cook until vegetables are tender, about 1 hour. Remove bay leaf before serving.

Ann's Raspberry Farm

Creamy Fall Fruit Soup

3 tablespoons butter
1 cup finely chopped onion
2 teaspoons pumpkin pie spice
1 teaspoon ground ginger
1 (15-ounce) can pumpkin
1 cup Cooper's Mill Chunky Applesauce
3½ cups chicken broth
¾ cup heavy cream
Apple chunks, optional

Melt butter in large saucepan on medium heat. Add onion; cook and stir 5 minutes or until softened. Stir in pumpkin pie spice and ginger. Stir in pumpkin, applesauce and broth until well blended and smooth. Bring to boil stirring occasionally. Reduce heat to low; simmer 5 minutes. Remove from heat. (For a smoother soup place soup in blender after cooked.) Stir in cream. Heat lightly before serving. If adding apples for a crunchy element, add apples at the same time as cream and stir.

Cooper's Mill Apple Butter & Jelly Factory

Spicy Tomato Soup

1 tablespoon oil
2 celery stalks, chopped
1 yellow onion, chopped
10 cloves garlic, minced
3 medium carrots, chopped
1 (109-ounce) can diced tomatoes
1 quart heavy whipping cream
3 tablespoons cumin
2 tablespoons celery salt
Tabasco sauce to taste

Add oil to large pot and turn on very low heat. Add celery, onion, garlic and carrots and cook till moisture appears on them (this is called sweating). Once moist, add diced tomatoes. Bring to a simmer for 30 minutes until the veggies are soft. Purée mixture in a blender and strain through a mesh strainer. Transfer to pot and add heavy cream, cumin, celery salt and Tabasco. Bring to a simmer until the flavors have developed, about 20 minutes.

Pyramid Hill Sculpture Park and Museum

1763 Hamilton Cleves Road • Hamilton, OH 45013
513-868-8336 • www.pyramidhill.org

Pyramid Hill Sculpture Park and Museum combines the lure of nature with the dynamic presence of monumental art. Located on over 300 acres of woodlands, gardens and lakes near Hamilton, Pyramid Hill is a unique experience to explore the countryside and marvel at over 60 pieces of outdoor art. Go go back in time at the indoor Ancient Sculpture Museum which houses Greek, Roman, Etruscan and Egyptian pieces. Drive through the rolling landscape, walk up to experience the sculpture, find a secluded picnic spot or hike a quiet trail through the forests. Pyramid Hill is a relaxing way to spend a day with art and nature.

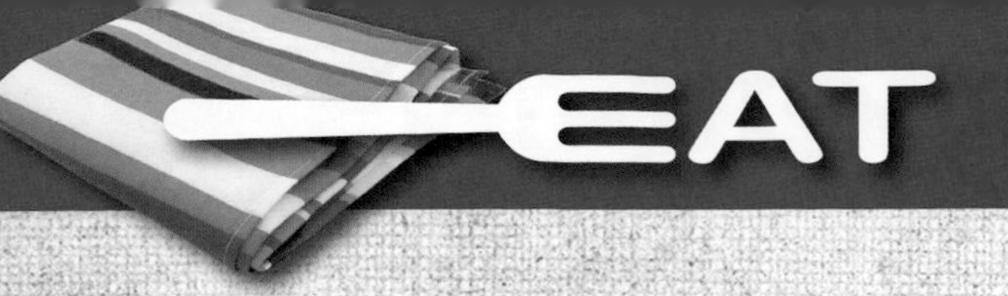

Tomato Bisque

2 tablespoons unsalted butter
2 medium onions, diced
4 cloves garlic, smashed and minced
2 (16-ounce) cans whole tomatoes
1 cup cold water
1 cup heavy cream
1 bay leaf
½ cup grated Parmesan cheese
½ cup brown sugar
Dash Tabasco sauce
Salt and pepper to taste

Heat a 6-quart stockpot. Add butter, and when it bubbles, add onions. Sauté onions until translucent. Add garlic and sauté until fragrant. Add tomatoes, water, cream and bay leaf. Bring to a simmer, reduce heat and cook 1 hour. Remove from heat, remove bay leaf and purée soup very well in batches in a blender. Return soup to pot and return to stove. Add cheese, brown sugar and Tabasco. Season to taste with salt, fresh pepper and more brown sugar if necessary. This soup should be very creamy and slightly sweet.

Chef Joshua Catone at Murphin Ridge Inn
Adams County Travel and Visitors Bureau

Historic Murphin Ridge Inn

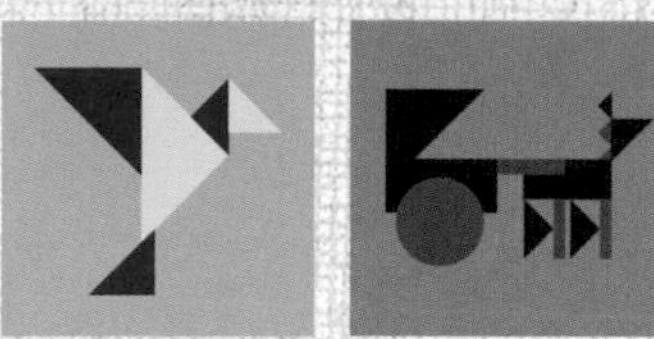

Adams
COUNTY, OH
Travel & Visitors Bureau

Adams County Travel and Visitors Bureau

509 East Main Street
West Union, OH 45693
877-232-6764
www.adamscountytravel.org

A visit to Adams County is a must for yearly travels. Stay at one of the classy Bed & Breakfast Inns or cabin nestled in the woods. Have a hearty breakfast before visiting the Wheat Ridge Amish Community, and take a drive to Serpent Mound. Adams County is full of mom and pop restaurants and dairy bars for a great lunch stop. Drive through the rural countryside to see the colorful barn quilts. To see the original, take State Route 247 south of West Union and look for the Ohio Star. Hiking trails at Edge of Appalachia Preserve begged to be explored. For a great picnic with a view, check out Creeks Bend on Waggoner Riffle Road or Adams Lake. There are tons of fun festivals for times of celebration. The Wheat Ridge Herb Fair, Caraway's Pumpkin Days, The Old Fashion Draft Horse Mule & Pony Days, Heritage Days, Jack Roush Day and Miller's Anniversary are all great events.

Captain Bailey's Seafood Chowder

½ pound bacon, diced into ¼-inch pieces
1 large red onion, chopped
4 carrots, diced
3 stalks celery, diced
½ cup diced green bell pepper
3 tablespoons finely chopped fresh parsley
1 (16-ounce) can diced tomatoes
2 medium potatoes, cut in ½-inch cubes
1 (8-ounce) jar clam juice
2 cups water
1 tablespoon garlic powder
½ teaspoon crushed red pepper
1 teaspoon white pepper
1 teaspoon black pepper
1 teaspoon thyme
1 bay leaf
3 (10-ounce) cans baby clams packed in water or 3 (6½-ounce) cans chopped clams, drained and rinsed thoroughly
16 ounces frozen salad shrimp
8 ounces fresh chopped crabmeat, optional

Cook bacon over medium heat until fat is rendered. Add onion and cook with bacon and bacon fat until translucent. Add carrots, celery, bell pepper and parsley and cook 10 minutes. In stockpot place bacon, bacon grease, vegetables and parsley. Add tomatoes, potatoes, clam juice and water. Add remaining spices, stirring thoroughly between each spice. Cook, uncovered, over medium-low heat until vegetables are tender, about 2 hours. Allow to cool. Reheat and bring pot to low boil. Add seafood. Reduce to medium heat and cook 10 minutes. Serve with oyster crackers.

Hocking Hills Tourism Association

Creamy Chicken Noodle Soup

Stock:
1 onion, quartered
2 carrots, rough chopped
2 stalks celery, rough chopped
1 whole head garlic, cut in half horizontally
4 skinless, boneless chicken breasts

Soup:
1 medium white onion, diced
4 carrots, diced
4 stalks celery, diced
6 ounces sliced mushrooms, optional
1 tablespoon garlic powder
1 teaspoon white pepper
1 teaspoon black pepper
1 teaspoon dried parsley
1 (26-ounce) can cream of chicken soup, or equivalent
1 (12-ounce) package Reames frozen homemade noodles

Place quartered onion, rough-chopped carrots, rough-chopped celery and garlic in stockpot. Place chicken breasts on top and cover with water. Cook over medium-high heat until chicken is tender and shreds easily (about 1 hour). Remove chicken from pot; set aside. Strain stock, discarding vegetables, return stock to pot.

To stockpot add diced vegetables and sliced mushrooms. Add spices and parsley, stirring thoroughly between each addition. Add cream of chicken soup and stir until completely absorbed into liquid. Shred chicken and add to pot. Cook, covered, over medium-low heat until vegetables are tender, about 2 hours. Add uncooked noodles during last hour of cooking.

Hocking Hills Tourism Association

Corn Chowder

6 to 8 slices bacon
½ cup butter, divided
3 large onions, chopped
¼ green bell pepper, diced
8 medium potatoes, peeled
  and diced
4 cups milk
½ cup cream
5 cups fresh corn kernels, cooked
¼ cup minced parsley
½ to 1 teaspoon nutmeg
1 teaspoon salt
½ teaspoon pepper

Fry bacon in skillet; when crisp, remove to paper towels to cool. Reserve 2 tablespoons bacon fat in skillet; add ¼ cup butter and onions and sauté over medium heat until tender. Add green bell pepper and sauté 2 to 3 minutes. Remove from heat. Cook potatoes in boiling water until tender; drain well. Combine milk and cream in a large saucepan and heat slowly. When warm, add onion mixture, potatoes, corn, parsley, nutmeg, salt and pepper. Bring to a simmer, remove from heat and let stand at least 3 hours to thicken. Before serving, warm soup and stir in remaining ¼ cup butter. Thin with milk if it is too thick. Garnish each bowl with crumbled bacon. Makes 12 servings.

Esther McCoy, Food Editor, Steubenville Herald Star
Historic Fort Steuben

Corn Chowder would have been a family meal served when the Land Office was a home/office in Steubenville in the early 19th century.

Historic Fort Steuben & Visitor Center

120 South 3rd Street • Steubenville, OH 43952
740-283-1787 • www.oldfortsteuben.com

History comes alive in Steubenville at a visit to Historic Fort Steuben—a fully reconstructed 18th century military fort on its original site overlooking the Ohio River. Visitors can tour eight buildings in the Fort as well as the original First Federal Land Office, a log structure dating from 1801. Learn about the early settlement of America, the Lewis and Clark expedition and other important events through changing displays and programs. The Visitor Center includes a gift shop and offers information on local attractions such as the Murals of Steubenville and the Pleasant Hill School House Museum. The city celebrates its heritage with Ohio Valley Frontier Days, the Greek Food Festival and the Dean Martin Festival.

Visitor Center is open all year, Monday through Friday, 10am to 4pm and on weekends, May through October.
Fort Steuben is open daily, May through October 10am to 4pm.

Old Man's Chili

1 yellow onion, divided
3 jalapeños, divided
2 cloves garlic
1 ghost chili pepper, optional
1 tablespoon cooking oil
1 pound spicy breakfast sausage
1 pound ground beef
2 tablespoons chili powder, divided
1 (15-ounce) can black beans
2 (15-ounce) cans chili beans
2 (10-ounce) cans Rotel
2 slices thick-cut bacon
1 orange bell pepper
1 (12-ounce) can Coca-Cola
1 tablespoon cumin
⅛ cup sugar
Sharp Cheddar cheese, grated
Ritz crackers

Dice ½ onion, 1 jalapeño, garlic and ghost chili pepper, if using. Place in skillet over low heat with oil. Add sausage and ground beef to skillet and turn to medium heat. Lightly cover with 1 tablespoon chili powder and brown. Drain. Empty all canned items except Coca-Cola into a large chili pot and turn to medium heat, stirring occasionally. Cut bacon into small strips with kitchen scissors and add to skillet.

Coarsely cut remaining onion, jalapeños and bell pepper and add to chili pot. Pour approximately ¼ can Coca-Cola into skillet and cook 5 minutes, then add to chili pot. Pour remaining Coca-Cola into chili pot.

Add remaining chili powder, cumin and sugar. Bring to a boil, then cool for 20 minutes. Bring back to a boil, then cool to serving temperature. Garnish with shredded Cheddar and Ritz crackers.

Dannie Devol
Old Man's Cave Chalets

Old Man's Cave Chalets

18905 State Route 664 South • Logan, OH 43138
740-385-6517 • www.oldmanscavechalets.com

With its majestic waterfalls, stunning peaks, diverse forests, and breath taking rock formations, there is no other location in Ohio like the Hocking Hills. Old Man's Cave Chalets is the original and premier cabin resort in the Hocking Hills area. Enjoy breathtaking scenery and more than 50 luxurious private cabins, lodges and cozy suites in secluded and lush wood settings each with their own private hot tub. Discover their four impressive lodges which accommodate 14 to 20 people, each with their own swimming pool. Minutes from the caves, state parks, zip lining, canoeing, horseback riding, shopping, and dining. Visit their web site for special romance and family packages or for a perfect Hot Tub Getaway.

White Chicken Chili

1 large onion, chopped
1 tablespoon vegetable oil
2 (4.5-ounce) cans chopped green chiles
2 teaspoons minced garlic
2 teaspoons ground cumin
1½ teaspoons dried oregano
½ teaspoon black pepper
¼ teaspoon salt
⅛ teaspoon ground red pepper
6 (15-ounce) cans Great Northern beans, drained
48 ounces chicken broth
1 medium bay leaf
5 cups cooked and chopped chicken breast
2 tablespoons chopped fresh cilantro
Monterey Jack cheese
Salsa
Sour cream
Chopped fresh cilantro
Crushed tortilla chips

Sauté onion in hot oil in large pot over medium-high heat until onion is tender. Add green chiles, garlic, cumin, oregano, black pepper, salt and red pepper; sauté 1 minute. Add beans, chicken broth and bay leaf. Bring to a boil, cover and reduce heat. Simmer, stirring occasionally, 30 minutes until beans are tender. Stir in chicken and simmer, stirring occasionally, 30 minutes until heated through. Remove bay leaf; stir in 2 tablespoons chopped fresh cilantro. Spoon into bowls and top with Monterey Jack cheese, salsa, sour cream, chopped cilantro and crushed tortilla chips if desired.

EXPLORE

Cleveland Dragon Boat Festival

Third Saturday in September

Nautica Entertainment Complex
2000 Sycamore Street • Cleveland, OH 44113
216-221-1389 • www.cledba.org

Having a storied tradition with Asian roots that dates more than 2,500 years, dragon boat racing takes place annually on the West Bank of the Cuyahoga River in Cleveland's historic Flats. The Cleveland Dragon Boat Festival is an excellent recreational sport for men and women of all ages and fitness levels. Dragon Boat racing incorporates high energy, fitness, team building and recreational exercise in a fun and competitive atmosphere. The 500 meter races are accomplished through team work, and the races have been touted as one of the best local events, year after year.

Smokey Mariner's Chili

1 pound lean ground beef
1 package maple breakfast sausage links (10 links), chopped
1 cup beef broth
⅓ cup hickory-style barbecue sauce
Dash liquid smoke, optional
1 (14-ounce) can kidney beans
1 (10.75-ounce) can red chili beans in sauce
1 (15-ounce) can tomato sauce
1 (14.5-ounce) can diced tomatoes
1 large onion, diced
½ cup diced celery
Dash chili powder

Brown ground beef in a small skillet; drain grease. Place remaining ingredients in a large stockpot. Add ground beef. Simmer until all ingredients are heated through.

Maritime Museum of Sandusky

5-Hour Movie Night Stew

2 pounds round steak, fat trimmed
6 carrots, cut in 1-inch pieces
2 (8-ounce) cans tomato sauce with cheese
½ medium-sized green bell pepper, chopped
1 cup water
1 cup coarsely chopped celery
1½ teaspoons salt
1 medium onion, chopped
¼ teaspoon pepper
1 slice white bread
3 to 4 large red potatoes, cut into eighths

Cut round steak into 1-inch pieces. Combine all ingredients in Dutch oven. Bake, tightly covered, in preheated oven at 250° for 5 hours.

Mary Beth Medford
Canton Palace Theatre

Irish Beef Stew

¼ cup vegetable oil
1¼ pounds stew beef, cut into 1-inch pieces
6 large garlic cloves, minced
8 cups beef stock or canned beef broth
2 tablespoons tomato paste
1 tablespoon sugar
1 tablespoon dried thyme
1 tablespoon Worcestershire sauce
2 bay leaves
2 tablespoons butter
3 pounds russet potatoes, peeled, cut into ½-inch pieces
1 large onion, chopped
4 carrots peeled, cut into ½-inch pieces (2 cups)
2 tablespoons chopped fresh parsley

Heat oil in heavy large pot over medium-high heat. Add beef and sauté until brown on all sides, about 5 minutes. Add garlic and sauté 1 minute. Add beef stock, tomato paste, sugar, thyme, Worcestershire sauce and bay leaves. Stir to combine. Bring mixture to boil. Reduce heat to medium-low, then cover and simmer 1 hour, stirring occasionally. Meanwhile, melt butter in another large pot over medium heat. Add potatoes, onion and carrots. Sauté vegetables until golden, about 20 minutes. Add vegetables to beef stew. Simmer uncovered until vegetables and beef are very tender, about 40 minutes. Discard bay leaves. Tilt pan and spoon off fat. Transfer stew to serving bowl. Sprinkle with parsley and serve.

Fitzgerald's Irish Bed & Breakfast

Picnic Macaroni Cheese Salad

1 (16-ounce) box small macaroni shells
1 (16-ounce) jar Cheez Whiz
1 large green bell pepper, seeded and chopped
1 large onion, chopped
1 large red pepper, seeded and chopped
2 medium tomatoes, chopped
Celery seed to taste
Salt and pepper to taste

Cook macaroni according to package directions. Drain, stir in Cheez Whiz while macaroni is still warm. Allow to cool; add chopped vegetables and stir. Add some celery seed, salt and pepper .

This is great for picnics because it does not need to be kept cold.

Sharon Manson, Waverly
Wine Tasting & Art Show

Jingle Bell Luminary Weekend

Weekend before Thanksgiving
www.piketravel.com

While visiting Waverly for the Wine Tasting & Art Show (see page 45) at Grand Restaurant & Tavern, enjoy local color during Jingle Bell Luminary Weekend. This festival features the Candy Cane Variety, quilt show, book sale, juried craft show, lantern tour with period costumed actors, museum programs, 5K Run, wine tasting, art show, many added attractions each year, and the largest night time illuminated Christmas Parade in Southern Ohio.

Dill Potato Salad

6 medium red potatoes, washed
1 cup sour cream
2 tablespoons chopped fresh dill
¼ cup finely chopped yellow bell pepper
½ cup chopped celery
½ cup chopped red sweet onion
Salt and pepper to taste

Boil potatoes until tender, about 30 minutes; drain, peel and dice. In separate bowl combine sour cream, dill, bell pepper, celery, onion, salt and pepper. In a large bowl, mix warm potatoes with dressing. Chill at least 2 hours before serving.

Gertrude Rasor
Columbus Park of Roses

Corn Salad Relish

1 tablespoon ground mustard
1 teaspoon celery seed, optional
1 teaspoon turmeric
1 quart vinegar
Salt to taste
12 ears tender yellow corn, kernels cut from cob
1 quart (4 cups) chopped cabbage
6 onions, chopped
3 sweet red bell peppers, chopped
3 green bell peppers, chopped

Make a solution of vinegar, mustard, celery seed, turmeric and salt; bring to full boil. Mix in vegetables and return to full boil. Pack in sterilized jars and seal. Makes about 6 pints. Use as a relish or as a salad.

Sweet Corn Festival

Cranberry Salad

1 (6-ounce) package cranberry flavored Jell-O mix
2 cups boiling water
½ orange, peeled and chopped
½ pound fresh or frozen cranberries, chopped
3 apples, peeled, cored and chopped
1 cup white sugar
1 cup chopped celery
1 cup chopped walnuts

Dissolve gelatin in boiling water. Refrigerate half an hour or until it begins to gel. Mix together orange, cranberries, apples and sugar. In a 9x13-inch dish, mix gelatin, fruit mixture, celery and walnuts. Chill 3 to 4 hours, until firm.

Destination Hilliard

Destination Hilliard

5274 Norwich Street • Hilliard, OH 43026
614-664-3290
www.destinationhilliard.com

Hilliard offers unique home town charm and hospitality just minutes from Columbus, Ohio. Visit historic treasurers, dine at local restaurants and experience fun events. Hilliard is a vibrant culinary community with chefs and entrepreneurs who have started local restaurants, which perfectly complements the rich heritage of the community. Unique attractions include the only Early Television Museum in the United States, authentic Historic Village, First Responders Park, Ten Pin Alley and Packrat Comics. The Franklin County Fair takes place for eight days each year in July. History comes alive at the Historical Village at Weaver Park especially during Heritage Day in October and Olde Hilliard Christmas during the month of December. For outdoor enthusiasts and those seeking adventure there is the Heritage Rail Trail and 31 miles of bike and running paths, the second most miles of central Ohio communities.

Winter Fruit Salad

1 apple, cored and cut into ½-inch pieces
1 pear, cored and cut into ½-inch pieces
2 Fuyu persimmons, stem and leaves cut out and cut into ½-inch pieces
2 mandarin oranges, peeled and segments separated
2 figs, stems removed and cut into small slices
Seeds from 1 pomegranate
Favorite The Olive Scene dark balsamic vinegar: Vanilla, Dark Chocolate, Tangerine, Fig, Cinnamon Pear, or Pomegranate

Combine fruit in a medium bowl. Drizzle a few tablespoons of balsamic vinegar over salad. Toss to mix.

The Olive Scene

The Olive Scene

5512 Liberty Avenue
Vermilion, OH 44089
440-963-0504
www.theolivescene.com

The Olive Scene, named Mainstreet Business of the Year 2014 by Heritage Ohio, is a unique tasting emporium of the world's finest Extra Virgin Olive Oils and Balsamic Vinegars with locations in Rocky River, Vermilion, and Chagrin Falls.

The olive oils are carefully pressed for quality, not quantity, so their flavor profiles and health benefits are exceptional. Every one of the olive oils are fresh, following the growing seasons of olives in the northern and southern hemispheres. The producers are setting the bar on the technique of harvesting and pressing olives in order to yield the freshest, healthiest, tastiest extra virgin olive oils on the market today.

The balsamic vinegars are from Modena, Italy, and are barrel aged with a wonderful balance of tart and sweet. Their full, sweet, zesty flavors make them perfect in vinaigrettes, sauces and soups or drizzled as a finish on vegetables, fish, meat and especially desserts. Come in and discover just how good healthy can taste.

Chicken Salad

5 pounds boneless, skinless chicken breasts
3 cups chopped celery
3 cups quartered red grapes
1 cup chopped walnuts
Mayonnaise
2 ounces lemon Juice

Boil chicken until it reaches 185° and remove to cool. When cool chop into approximately ⅜-inch pieces. Add celery, red grapes and walnuts. Add enough mayonnaise to moisten all ingredients. Add lemon juice. Chill all and serve cold.

Susie's Big Dipper

Susie's Big Dipper

323 North Main Street
Piqua, OH 45356
937-615-0700
www.susiesbigdipper.com

Susie's Big Dipper is a modern-day, old-fashioned Ice cream parlor and café filled with a small-town, fun, family atmosphere. Purchased in 2010, Susie and Wayne started making their own ice cream right in the basement and all their soups and sandwiches in a tiny little kitchen. All the sandwiches and soups are offered on or with fresh homemade bread. Creations such as the latest ice cream named Chocolate Overload bring people back for more. Being the only place in Miami County that makes homemade, hand-dipped gourmet ice cream, they now make more than 30 flavors of which 24 are offered daily. People come from miles around to indulge in the tasty treats. They expanded their offerings by going mobile allowing them to bring their creations anywhere such as parties and festivals. It will be well worth a trip to check out this hometown eatery in downtown Piqua, Ohio.

Buffalo Chicken Salad

Mixed greens
1 hardboiled egg, diced
Sliced tomatoes
¼ red onion, sliced thin
Chicken strips, grilled or fried
Buffalo sauce
Cheddar cheese
Ranch dressing

Place mixed greens on a plate. Add diced egg, sliced tomatoes and red onion. Place chicken strips in bowl and toss with buffalo sauce until well coated. Top salad with chicken and sprinkle with shredded Cheddar cheese. Serve with ranch dressing.

HideAway Country Inn

1601 State Route 4
Bucyrus, OH 44820
419-562-3013
www.hideawayinn.com

Top 10 Romantic Inn in USA 2015*

12 Private Double whirlpool Suites - 8 with fireplaces, Award Winning Chef, FREE Wifi, FREE Full Breakfast

Wine Spectator Award of Excellence Wine Cellar, Full Service Spa

Private Dining, Fine Casual Locally Sourced Scratch Kitchen

6 acres of Pristine Gardens, Hammocks, and life- sized Games

Heart of Ohio - Located Between Cleveland, Columbus and Toledo, Ohio.

Easy To Find... Hard to Leave Award Winning Bouquet Hotel

Buttermilk Coleslaw

6 cups shredded cabbage
½ medium green bell pepper, chopped fine
½ cup shredded carrot
⅛ teaspoon celery seed
1 or 2 stalks celery, diced, optional

Combine all ingredients; mix well.

Dressing:

1 cup mayonnaise
¾ cup buttermilk
¼ cup sugar
Salt and pepper to taste

In separate bowl combine all Dressing ingredients; mix well. Add to vegetable mixture and toss, coating well. Let marinate at least 30 minutes prior to serving.

Canal Winchester Blues & Ribfest

First Friday and Saturday in August

Downtown Canal Winchester

10 North High Street • Canal Winchester, OH 43110

614-270-5053 • www.bluesandribfest.com

The air is filled with barbecue wood smoke and the timeless beat of authentic American Blues at Ohio's only Blues & Rib Festival. This two day summer street celebration features live blues music, world-class ribs, a variety of quality non-rib food options, children's activities, fan-cooled dining areas, and a beer and wine garden. From solid rockin' electric blues to traditional acoustic performances, there's something sure to satisfy even the most discriminating blues fan continuously flowing from two stages throughout the two-day event. Bring friends, an appetite, and a couple of lawn chairs for one of the best parties of the summer! Families are welcome and admission is free.

Perfection Salad

This is a favorite salad from the 1960's served by the ladies at Wapakoneta, St. Paul United Church of Christ, Neil Armstrong's home church.

2 (6-ounce) packages lime Jell-O
4 cups hot water
3 cups cold water
2 cups shredded cabbage
½ cup grated carrot
¼ cup shredded celery
1 cup crushed pineapple, drained
1 (3-ounce) package lemon Jell-O

Combine lime Jell-O with 4 cups hot water in a large bowl, stirring until dissolved. Stir in cold water. Add vegetables and drained pineapple. Pour mixture into a metal or silicone mold (rinse first in cold water) or serving dish. Refrigerate until set, 2 or 3 hours. Prepare lemon Jell-O per package directions. Pour over first mixture after it has set. Refrigerate several hours or overnight. Unmold by dipping into hot water 10 seconds.

Armstrong Air & Space Museum

Brussels Sprout Salad

4 tablespoons minced onion
4 tablespoons olive oil
2 tablespoons Ann's Raspberry Farm's Hungarian Hot Mustard
2 tablespoons balsamic vinegar
2 cloves garlic, minced
¼ teaspoon salt
½ teaspoon black pepper
½ pound Brussels sprouts, thinly sliced
¼ cup toasted pecans, chopped
¼ cup blue cheese, crumbled
6 slices bacon, cooked and crumbled, optional

Combine onion, olive oil, hot mustard, balsamic vinegar, garlic, salt and pepper to create salad dressing. Pour dressing over raw Brussels sprouts and toss to coat. Blend in chopped nuts and crumbled cheese. Chill 1 hour. Top with crispy bacon and serve.

Ann's Raspberry Farm

Avocado, Bacon and Seared Scallop Salad with Chipotle Vinaigrette

Salad:

2 slices bacon per person, cut into matchsticks
3 to 4 fresh sea scallops per person
Salt and pepper to taste
Mixed greens
¼ avocado per person, sliced

Chipotle Vinaigrette:

1 part chipotle oil (about 1 tablespoon per person)
1 part fresh lemon or lime juice (about 1 tablespoon per person)
Pinch salt (smoked sea salt would be perfect)
Cracked fresh pepper

Crisp bacon over medium heat in a frying pan. Remove bacon, leave fat in pan. Season scallops with salt and pepper. Sear over medium-high heat in bacon fat. It should only take between 1½ to 3 minutes per side. Do not overcook, they will become tough. Make vinaigrette by whisking chipotle oil slowly into lemon juice. Add salt and pepper and adjust seasonings to taste. Toss greens with vinaigrette and lay a bed of greens on a plate. Arrange bacon, avocado and scallops on top of greens. Crack some fresh pepper on top and enjoy.

The Olive Scene

The Inn's House Salad

4 to 5 thin slices red onion
2 cups ice water
3 tablespoons champagne vinaigrette dressing, divided
4 to 5 clementine oranges, peeled and wedge sliced
3 ounces arugula
3 ounces fresh spinach
1 tablespoon extra virgin olive oil
¼ cup dried cranberries
3 ounces crumbled blue cheese

Add thinly sliced red onion to ice water. Soak 15 minutes to reduce astringency. Drain. Add onions to small, dry bowl along with 1 tablespoon champagne vinaigrette dressing. Add clementine oranges to bowl and mix well. Combine arugula and fresh spinach in separate large bowl. Add remaining champagne vinaigrette dressing and olive oil. Mix and combine. Plate salad plates with arugula-spinach mixture. Arrange red onions, clementine oranges and cranberries on top. Sprinkle with crumbled blue cheese to taste and serve.

Welsh Hills Inn

Broccoli Salad Supreme

2 heads broccoli, cut into bite-size pieces
1 small head cauliflower, cut into bite-size pieces
1 small red onion, sliced
1 cup shredded sharp Cheddar cheese, optional
1 pound bacon, fried until crisp and crumbled
1 cup raisins, optional
1 cup mayonnaise
½ cup sugar
6 tablespoon cider vinegar
1 tablespoon bacon drippings

Combine broccoli, cauliflower, onion, cheese, bacon and raisins. Mix well. In a separate bowl, combine mayonnaise, sugar, vinegar and bacon drippings. Pour over broccoli mixture, mix well and chill before serving.

Gertrude Rasor
Columbus Park of Roses

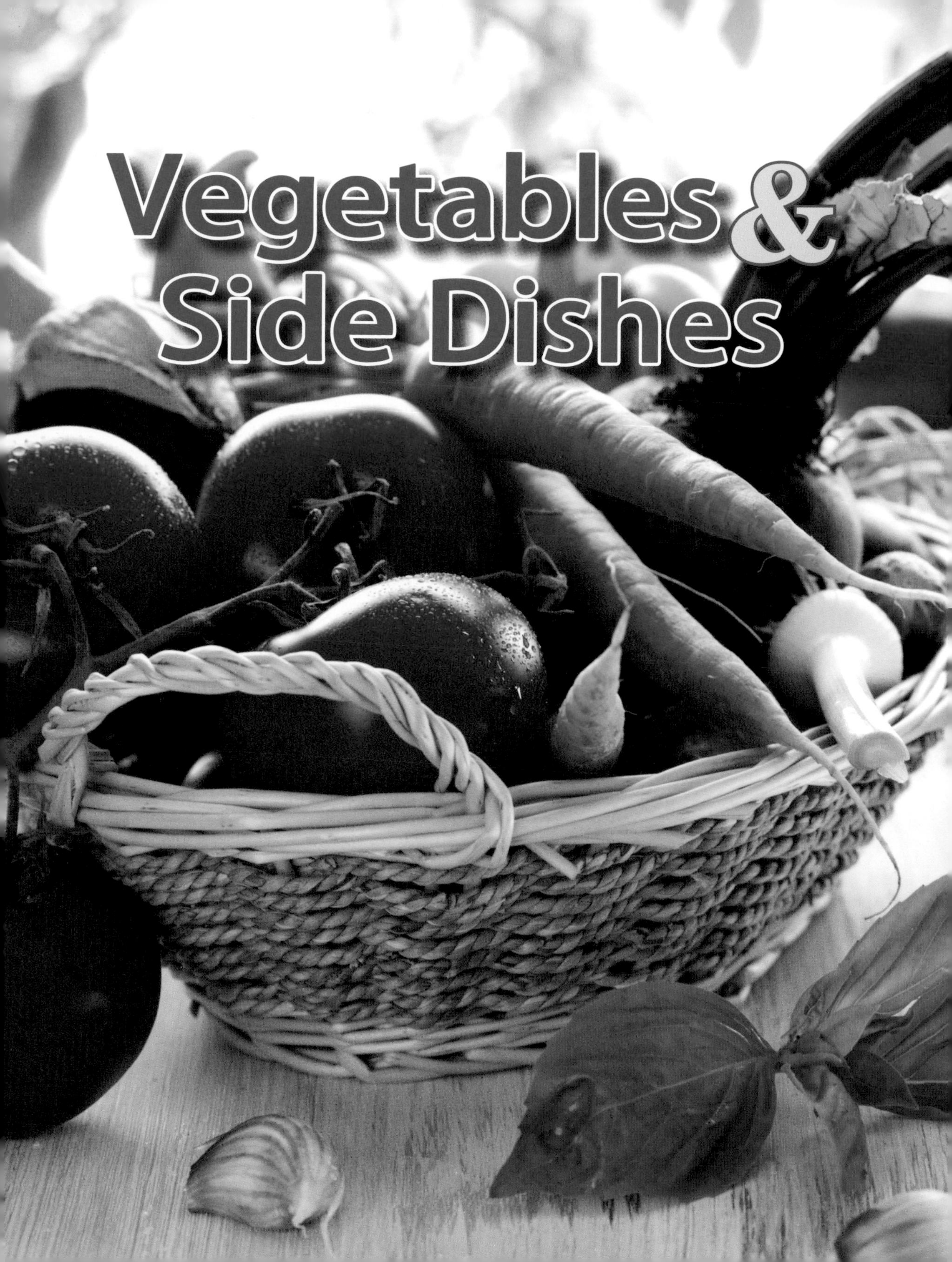

Vegetables & Side Dishes

Baked Corn Casserole

4 to 5 ears Witten's sweet corn
1 (15-ounce) can cream-style corn
8 ounces sour cream
2 eggs, beaten
1 (8.5-ounce) box corn muffin mix
1 stick butter, melted

Boil ears of corn 15 minutes and cut off the cob. Combine corn with remaining ingredients and pour into lightly greased 2½-quart casserole dish. Bake at 350° for 55 to 60 minutes.

Note: May substitute 1 (15-ounce) can whole-kernel corn for the fresh ears.

The Witten Farm Market & Greenhouse

The Witten Farm Market & Greenhouse

16670 State Route 60 • Lowell, OH 45744
740-984-4009 • 740-984-2059 • www.WittenFarm.com

This 3rd generation family owned farm is located on the sandy banks of the Muskingum River in Lowell, Ohio. They grow over 300 acres of sweet corn and 150 acres of other fruits and vegetables, including strawberries, tomatoes, cantaloupe, green beans, peppers, cucumbers and squash. They also have Sweet Georgia Peaches and Juicy Watermelon to satisfy sweet summer cravings. To get the produce from field to fork as quick as possible, they have hit the road to set up 22 satellite farm markets across southeastern and central Ohio and West Virginia. Look for the produce wagons with the red and white striped awnings. Open May through September, the Witten Farm Market & Greenhouse offers a convenient way to enjoy fresh from the farm produce on a daily basis. Visit the website to learn more about the fresh produce and one-of a-kind hanging baskets and specialty containers available during the spring.

Corn Pudding

3 tablespoons butter
3 eggs
2 teaspoons sugar
1 teaspoon salt
1 heaping teaspoon flour
6 ears corn, shucked and kernels cut off
1 pint milk

Mix butter, eggs, sugar, salt, flour and corn kernels; beat thoroughly. Add milk and stir well. Bake at 350° for 1 hour.

Sweet Corn Festival

Sweet Corn Festival

Admission is free • Historic Lions Park
2900 Chautauqua Boulevard • Millersport, OH 43046
740-467-3639 • www.sweetcornfest.com

Wednesday through Saturday before Labor Day
Wednesday through Friday 5pm to 11pm and Saturday 11am to 11pm

Enjoy hot dripping ears of sweet corn, a large midway, tractor pulls, square dancing, contests, clogging, heritage village, and lots of festive foods. The festivities kick off with the Grand parade on Wednesday at 6:00pm. The always popular Nashville country music shows are on Friday and Saturday at 8:30pm. The 5K run starts with a bang on Saturday at 9:00am. Come see why it is "Earresistible!"

Sponsored by the Millersport Lions Club

Corn Pudding

3½ cups fresh sweet corn, scraped from cob (about 6 or 7 ears)
1 tablespoon flour
3 eggs
1 cup heavy cream
½ cup milk
1 tablespoons sugar
½ teaspoon salt
1 teaspoon baking powder
3 tablespoons butter, melted

In large bowl, toss corn with flour. In separate bowl, beat together eggs, heavy cream, milk, sugar, salt and baking powder. Stir in melted butter. Pour into corn-flour mixture and stir well. Lightly grease a 2-quart oven-safe casserole. Ladle corn into casserole. Set casserole into large baking pan filled with ½ inch of water. Bake at 375° for 20 to 30 minutes, until a knife inserted ½ inch from edge of dish comes out clean. Pudding should be golden on top and slightly puffed.

Peg Vodraska, owner
Rittman Orchards & Farm Market

Corn Pudding

⅔ cup flour
½ cup cornmeal
1 cup plus 3 tablespoons sugar
1 tablespoon baking powder
½ teaspoon salt
2 tablespoons oil
1 cup milk
1 (15-ounce) can whole-kernel corn
1 (15-ounce) can cream-style corn
1 cup sour cream
2 eggs
10 tablespoons butter, melted

Preheat oven to 350°. Combine all ingredients together. Place in 9x13-inch glass baking dish. Bake 25 to 30 minutes or until golden brown on top and around edges.

Market Street Inn

Zucchini Stuffing Casserole

4 medium zucchini, unpeeled, sliced ½-inch thick
6 tablespoons butter, divided
1 (10-ounce) can cream of chicken soup
½ cup sour cream
2½ cups herbed stuffing cubes, divided
¾ cup shredded carrots
½ cup chopped onion

Cook zucchini in boiling salted water till tender; drain. Remove from heat; stir in 3 tablespoons butter, soup, sour cream and 1½ cups stuffing cubes. Gently stir in carrots and onions. Turn into a greased 2½-quart casserole dish. Melt remaining 3 tablespoons butter, add to remaining 1 cup stuffing cubes, toss and place on top of casserole. Bake at 350° for 30 to 40 minutes.

The Barn Inn Bed and Breakfast

Greek Spaghetti Squash

1 spaghetti squash, halved lengthwise and seeded
2 tablespoons vegetable oil
1 onion, chopped
1 clove garlic, minced
1½ cups chopped tomatoes
¾ cup crumbled feta cheese
3 tablespoons sliced black olives
2 tablespoons chopped fresh basil

Preheat oven to 350°. Lightly grease a baking sheet. Place spaghetti squash with cut sides down on prepared baking sheet. Bake 30 minutes or until a sharp knife can be inserted with only a little resistance. Remove squash from oven and set aside to cool enough to be easily handled. Meanwhile, heat oil in a skillet over medium heat. Cook and stir onion in oil until tender. Add garlic; cook and stir until fragrant, 2 to 3 minutes. Stir in tomatoes and cook until tomatoes are warmed through. Use a large spoon to scoop the stringy pulp from the squash and place in a medium bowl. Toss with the vegetables, feta cheese, olives and basil. Serve warm.

Knox County Convention & Visitors Bureau

Honey Run Waterfall and Park

EXPLORE

Dan Emmett Music & Arts Festival

Knox County Convention & Visitors Bureau

800-837-5282

www.VisitKnoxOhio.org • www.TheWoodward.org

Knox County is proud of its rich heritage, and visitors will take pleasure in it, too. Visitors will find themselves whistling the tune of "Dixie," composed by local musician Daniel Decatur Emmett, or find they get lost in a playful state of mind like homegrown comedian/actor Paul Lynde. There are juicy apples dangling from trees likely descended from seeds planted by Johnny Appleseed himself. Harvest@TheWoodward, a hometown local foods grocery and handcrafted gift shop, celebrates the best products that central Ohio has to offer. Whether in the mood for delicious meats, cheeses, or something to satisfy a sweet tooth, the Harvest provides high-quality, locally produced food and outstanding customer service. From Fredericktown to Martinsburg, from Danville to Centerburg, to the heart of it all in Mount Vernon, there are smiling faces and warm welcomes in Knox County.

Spaghetti Basil Torte

1 (16-ounce) package spaghetti
½ cup grated Parmesan cheese
½ cup ricotta cheese
1 tablespoon Italian seasoning
2 eggs, beaten
¼ cup chopped fresh basil
2 medium tomatoes, each cut into 5 slices
4 (1-ounce) slices provolone cheese, cut in half

Preheat oven to 350°. Spray a 9-inch springform pan with cooking oil. Cook and drain spaghetti as directed on package. Rinse with cold water and drain. In a large bowl combine Parmesan cheese, ricotta cheese, Italian seasoning and eggs. Add cooked spaghetti and toss until well coated. Press half of mixture in bottom of pan. Sprinkle with half of the basil. Layer with half of the tomato and cheese slices. Press remaining spaghetti mixture on top. Sprinkle with remaining basil. Layer with remaining tomato and cheese slices.

Bake uncovered 30 minutes until hot and light brown. Let stand 15 minutes. Release side of pan. Cut into wedges.

The Alpacas of Spring Acres

Spring Acres B&B
at The Alpacas of Spring Acres

3370 Big-B Road • Zanesville, OH 43701
740-796-6904
www.TheAlpacasofspringacres.com
www.bedandbreakfast.com • www.justbedandbreakfast.net

Spring Acres B&B is a beautiful 4-bedroom guesthouse located on 180 acres of farmland, home to over 60 Suri Alpacas. Leave the busy world to wake up to the sound of nothing and the smell of breakfast. Come stay in the beautiful B&B, swim in or fish on the 5-acre lake, kick back and enjoy a good book on the outside deck, and take a tour of the farm to learn more about living the alpaca lifestyle. Spring Acres B&B is an ideal location for meetings, seminars, and parties.

Calico Beans

1 pound ground beef
1 medium sweet onion, diced
½ pound bacon, diced
½ cup ketchup
2 tablespoons vinegar
½ cup packed brown sugar
½ teaspoon garlic powder
1 (15-ounce) can pinto beans
1 (28-ounce) can Bush's baked beans
1 (15-ounce) can Great Northern beans
1 (15-ounce) can butter beans
1 (15-ounce) can kidney beans
1 (15-ounce) can navy beans
1 (7-ounce) can diced green chiles

Preheat oven to 350°. In a large pot, brown ground beef, onion and bacon. Drain and remove from heat. Stir in ketchup, vinegar, brown sugar and garlic powder, mixing well. Add beans and green chiles; stir. Pour into a large roasting pan or oven-safe baking dish. Bake 1 hour. Serve hot.

Long's Retreat Family Resort

50 Bell Hollow Road • Latham, OH 45646
937-588-3725 • www.longsretreat.com
www.facebook.com/longsretreat

Long's Retreat is camping, water, and recreation fun! We're located on over 400 acres of Southern Ohio's scenic hills, featuring spacious trailer and tent sites. Choose from shaded and lakeside sites, primitive, electric, and full hook-ups as well as cabin rentals. Water fun includes two giant waterslides, a beach swimming area with lifeguards, diving boards, a tube slide and splash pad, along with canoeing, paddle boating and fishing on our 20-acre private lake. There are also many recreational activities, such as miniature golf, adult and kiddie go karts, carousel, rock climbing wall, moon bounce, full court basketball, tennis, sand volleyball and a video arcade. Amenities include a camp store, two concession snack bars, hot showers, restroom facilities, laundromat, propane gas, security guards, playgrounds, shelter houses and picnic areas. Come and play for a day, a weekend, a week, or all season long!

Italian Green Beans

2 medium onions, thinly sliced into rings
¾ cup Italian dressing
2 (16-ounce) bag frozen green beans
1 (14.5-ounce) can diced tomatoes, drained
½ tablespoon salt
½ teaspoon pepper

In a large nonstick skillet brown onions very slightly in a dry skillet. Add salad dressing and sauté about 3 minutes. Add green beans, tomatoes and seasoning; mix well. Cover and cook until beans are tender, about 10 minutes. Serve hot. Serves 6 to 8.

Sweet Onion Bake

5 medium Vidalia onions, sliced ¼ inch thick
½ stick margarine
½ sleeve saltine cracker, crushed (plus a few more for topping)
1 (10.75-ounce) can cream of mushroom soup
2 eggs, beaten
½ cup milk
1½ cups shredded Cheddar cheese

Treat a 2-quart casserole with nonstick spray. Melt margarine in a skillet over medium heat; sauté onions until clear and tender. Sprinkle cracker crumbs in bottom of dish. Layer onions over crackers. Combine soup, eggs and milk. Pour over onions. Combine cheese and about 5 crushed crackers. Sprinkle over top of casserole. Bake at 350° for 30 minutes or until brown and bubbly. Serves 6.

Baked Mushroom Casserole

A delicious make-ahead dish.

1½ pounds mushrooms, sliced
4 tablespoons butter
½ cup diced celery
½ cup diced green bell pepper
½ cup diced onion
½ cup mayonnaise
½ loaf French bread, cubed
1 (10.75-ounce) can cream of mushroom soup
3 eggs
1 teaspoon salt
½ teaspoon pepper
1 cup shredded Cheddar cheese

Sauté mushrooms in butter. Add celery, bell pepper and onion and sauté until soft. Drain well. Combine mayonnaise, bread and soup. Add mushroom mixture and pout into a treated 2-quart casserole. Combine eggs, salt and pepper; pour over top of casserole. Refrigerate overnight. Bake at 350° for 1 hour topping with cheese the last 10 minutes of bake time.

Roasted Cauliflower

1 head cauliflower, cut into bite-size florets
2 tablespoons extra-virgin olive oil

Preheat oven to 425°. On a baking sheet, toss cauliflower with olive oil; season with salt and pepper and arrange in an even layer. Roast until tender and browned, 20 to 25 minutes.

Recipe provide by Covered Bridge Gardens
Ashtabula Covered Bridge Festival

Ashtabula Covered Bridge Festival

October

Downtown Jefferson and at the 18 covered bridges

25 West Jefferson Street • Jefferson, OH 44047

440-576-3769 •www.coveredbridgefestival.org

There are 18 covered bridges in Ashtabula County, and every year during the Covered Bridge Festival they are beautifully decorated for fall. There is the main festival downtown in Jefferson, and there are events at many of the bridges. During the festival there is a Queen's pageant, a parade, entertainment, crafters, food vendors, beautiful scenery and the longest and shortest covered bridge in the U.S.

Oscar's Vegetable Casserole

2 (15-ounce) cans Veg-All, drained
1 medium onion, diced
4 ounces shredded Cheddar cheese
1 (8-ounce) can water chestnuts, drained
1 cup Hellmann's mayonnaise
1 sleeve Ritz crackers, crushed
1 stick butter, melted

Combine Veg-All, onion, cheese, water chestnuts and mayonnaise; mix well and place in casserole dish. Cover with Ritz crackers. Pour butter over all. Bake at 350° for 30 minutes, uncovered.

Mary Beth Medford
Canton Palace Theatre

Canton Palace Theatre

605 Market Avenue North
Canton, OH 44702
330-454-8172
www.cantonpalacetheatre.org
Facebook: Canton Palace Theatre
Twitter: CantonPalaceTHR
Instagram: CantonPalaceTheatre

The Canton Palace Theatre is a 1489-seat historic, atmospheric theatre located in downtown Canton, Ohio. It first opened on November 23, 1926. The Canton Palace Theatre serves as both the literal and figurative cornerstone of the Downtown Canton Arts District. A vital multi-purpose entertainment facility, its marquee burns brightly 60 feet above Market Avenue, welcoming visitors to enter its grand foyer and become a part of Canton's nostalgic past. Hosting over 300 events (movies, concerts, comedy shows, dance performances, wedding ceremonies and receptions, private parties, and fundraisers) a year, with an attendance of over 100,000 guests, the Palace strives to be an important part of Canton's future.

Party Potatoes

1 (32-ounce) package frozen diced hash browns
½ medium yellow onion, finely chopped
1 (10-ounce) can cream of celery soup
1 cup milk
1 (8-ounce) package cream cheese
8 ounces shredded sharp Cheddar cheese

Place frozen potatoes in greased 9x13-inch glass baking dish. Sprinkle onion over potatoes. In saucepan combine soup, milk and cream cheese over medium heat until creamy. Pour mixture over potatoes. Cover with shredded cheese. Bake at 325° for 1 to 1½ hours. You may want to cover the dish with aluminum foil for first half hour so cheese does not get overdone. If you cover the dish spray foil with nonstick spray so cheese does not stick.

Hocking Hills Tourism Association

Hocking Hills

www.explorehockinghills.com

The Hocking Hills are Ohio's natural crown jewels, where unsurpassed beauty takes eco adventure seekers along miles of trails, waterfalls, prehistoric caves and spectacular cliff-top vistas. The surrounding natural wonders inspire a robust artist community. Galleries pepper the hills and antique malls delight treasure hunters. Music fills the hills May through September at family friendly festivals celebrating the history and Appalachian culture of the region.

Glazed Carrots

6 medium carrots, peeled and sliced ¼-inch thick on the bias
½ teaspoon salt
3 tablespoons sugar, divided
½ cup low-sodium chicken broth
3 tablespoons unsalted butter, cut into 4 pieces
2 teaspoons lemon juice

Bring carrots, salt, 1 tablespoon sugar and chicken broth to boil, covered, in 10-inch skillet over medium-high heat. Reduce heat to medium and simmer, stirring occasionally until carrots are almost tender when poked with tip of paring knife, about 5 minutes. Uncover, increase heat to high and simmer rapidly, stirring occasionally until liquid is reduced to about 2 tablespoons, about 1 to 2 minutes. Add butter and remaining 2 tablespoons sugar to skillet, toss carrots to coat and cook, stirring frequently until carrots are completely tender and glaze is light gold, about 3 minutes. Turn off heat, add lemon juice, toss to coat. Transfer carrots to serving dish, scraping glaze from pan. Season to taste with pepper and serve immediately.

Gertrude Rasor
Columbus Park of Roses

Columbus Park of Roses

3901 North High Street
Columbus, OH 43214
614-645-3391 • www.parkofroses.org

Rose peak bloom seasons: late May through June and late August through September

Free, open dawn to dusk year round, wheelchair accessible

Dedicated in 1953, this 13-acre city park contains 3 unique rose gardens and herb and perennial gardens. With 12,000 roses of 400+ varieties, it is among the largest public rose gardens in America. The main rose garden is classically designed, with a long mall, spacious walkways, symmetrical beds, rose-covered arbors, a fountain and tall viewing tower from which to see the entire garden. The heritage garden showcases fragrant, old fashioned roses and decorative shrubs. The EarthKind garden features hardy, low maintenance shrub and climbing roses interplanted with specimen trees. Many of these roses are right at home in modern residential gardens. In the herb garden, plants are grouped by usage, including medicinal, culinary, Native American and dye beds. The perennial garden features seasonally changing displays of flowers, ground covers and grasses and includes many native plants.

Lemon Bok Choy Stir-Fry

Pairs well with Trovato, Via Vecchia's smooth blend of Sangiovese & Pinot Noir.

5 to 6 cups baby bok choy
3 small heirloom carrots
1 teaspoon Himalayan pink sea salt
2 tablespoons extra virgin olive oil
⅓ cup cashews
½ tablespoon lemon juice

Chop bok choy and slice carrots into ½-inch chunks. Heat a shallow skillet; add oil and salt. Once pan is hot, combine all ingredients and stir-fry 10 to 15 minutes or until bok choy is soft.

Katrina Elmer
Via Vecchia Winery

Via Vecchia Winery

485 South Front Street • Columbus, OH 43215
614-886-2839 • www.ViaVecchiaWinery.com
Facebook: Via Vecchia Winery • Twitter: @ViaVecchiaVino
Instagram: ViaVecchiaWinery

Via Vecchia is a fully-functional urban winery in an historic 1800's building featuring exposed brick archways and wood ceiling beams. Whole grapes from the San Joaquin Valley in Lodi, California, are crafted into artisan wines by a vintner who follows an authentic Tuscan process, all in the heart of Columbus's Brewery District. Every October, the winery holds an annual grape crush of premium whole grapes imported from Lodi. Via Vecchia is dedicated to traditional winemaking using a single ingredient: grapes. The winery avoids modern methods of adding lab-cultured yeasts as well as other cellar treatments. Fermentation is brought on using natural yeasts that exist on the grape skins and within the environment. Via Vecchia also avoids additives of any sort excluding minimal sulfating to protect the wine during bottling. Wines are left unfiltered and age for a minimum of one year in French Oak barrels.

Broccoli Casserole

1 cup water
½ teaspoon salt
1 cup rice
¼ cup butter
¼ cup chopped onion
¼ cup chopped celery
1 (10-ounce) can cream of mushroom soup
1 (10-ounce) can cream of celery soup
1 (10-ounce) package frozen chopped broccoli, thawed
¼ cup cubed Velveeta cheese
1 (6-ounce) can French fried onions

Bring water and salt to a boil. Add rice; cover and remove from heat. Let set 5 minutes. Melt butter in skillet. Sauté onion and celery until tender. In large bowl combine rice, celery and onion with the soups, broccoli and cheese. Pour into a greased 2½-quart casserole dish. Top with French fried onions. Bake at 350° for 1 hour.

Charm Countryview Favorites: Famous Recipes from the Inn
Charm Countryview Inn

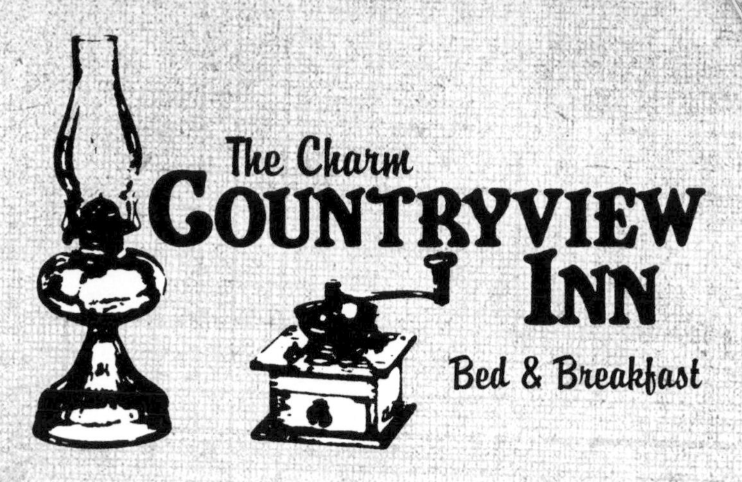

334 OH-557 • Baltic, OH 43804
330-893-3003 • www.charmcountryviewinn.com

The Charm Countryview Inn, a bed and breakfast Inn, is located 2.5 miles southeast of the small village of Charm, Ohio. The Inn perches on a quiet hillside overlooking peaceful country meadows and farms in Ohio's scenic Holmes County, home of the world's largest Amish community. The Inn is owned and operated by us, the Abe Mast Family. Many folks have made Charm Countryview Inn their second home. This Amish Country bed and breakfast is a place to relax, refresh the spirit, rejuvenate the mind and breathe in some pure Amish country air.

Peter's Baked Mac-n-Cheese

½ pound extra sharp Cheddar cheese
½ pound Gruyère Cheese
½ cup unsalted butter
½ cup flour
3 chicken bouillon cubes
1 teaspoon onion powder
½ teaspoon white pepper
1 teaspoon Beau Monde
½ teaspoon dry mustard
Dash cayenne pepper
Dash fresh ground nutmeg
4 cups whole milk
3 ounces shaved Parmesan cheese
Dash Lea & Perrins Worcestershire sauce
1 (16-ounce) package elbow macaroni, cooked al dente and drained
Paprika

Preheat oven to 350°. Grease a shallow, 2-quart baking dish. Cut Cheddar and Gruyère cheese into ½-inch cubes; set aside. Melt butter in saucepan. Add flour, bouillon cubes, onion powder, white pepper, Beau Monde, dry mustard, cayenne pepper and nutmeg to make a roux. Cook over low heat, stirring frequently until mixture is bubbly. Stir in milk. Cook until sauce is thick. Add cheese cubes slowly to the sauce stirring until melted. Add Parmesan cheese and Worcestershire sauce. Remove from heat. Stir in macaroni to coat well. Top with paprika to taste.

Peter Larson and Grand Ole Opry star, Minnie Pearl
Welsh Hills Inn

Slow Cooker Mac and Cheese

2 cups skim milk
1 (12-ounce) can evaporated milk
1 egg
1 teaspoon salt
¼ teaspoon pepper
1 cup frozen peas
1 tablespoon minced shallots
1½ cups shredded sharp Cheddar cheese
1 cup diced ham
2 cups uncooked elbow macaroni

Spray inside of slow cooker with nonstick spray. In a mixing bowl whisk together milk, evaporated milk, egg, salt and pepper. Pour milk mixture into slow cooker. Add peas, shallots, cheese, ham and uncooked macaroni. Stir gently to mix. Cook on low 3 to 4 hours, or until custard is set and the macaroni is tender. Do not cook more than 4 hours or the sides will begin to dry out. Serve immediately.

Destination Hilliard

Roasted Sweet Potatoes & Onions

2 sweet potatoes, sliced into ⅛-inch thick coins
1 onion, quartered then cut into ½-inch slices
2 tablespoons olive oil
Salt and pepper to taste

Preheat oven to 400°. Combine all ingredients in a large bowl. Toss to coat evenly, separating potato slices as needed. Line a baking sheet with aluminum foil or parchment paper for easy clean up. Transfer vegetables to baking sheet and spread in a single layer. Bake 20 to 30 minutes, or until onions begin to crisp and brown and sweet potatoes are cooked through.

The Olive Scene

Griddle Apple Rings

3 large cooking apples (Jonagold work extremely well)
¼ cup melted butter, divided
½ teaspoon lemon juice
¼ teaspoon cinnamon
1 tablespoon sugar

Preheat griddle. Wash and core apples; cut each into 4 crosswise slices. Combine 2 tablespoons of melted butter with lemon juice and brush on both sides of all apple rings. Cook approximately 1½ minutes, or until golden brown on the underside. Turn over. Add more butter as needed to prevent sticking. Grill 1½ minutes longer, or until tender. While rings are still on griddle, sprinkle with cinnamon and sugar. Serve.

Note: Can also be prepared using a stovetop skillet, but the griddle is a convenient way to cook all of the rings at once.

Peg Vodraska, owner
Rittman Orchards & Farm Market

Meat & Seafood

Meatballs

2 pounds ground beef
5 ounces evaporated milk
2 cups oats
½ cup chopped onion
2 to 3 teaspoons salt
½ teaspoon pepper
2 teaspoons chili powder
½ teaspoon garlic powder
2 eggs

Combine all ingredients. Form into golf ball-size balls, and place in 9x13-inch baking dish.

Sauce:

2 cups ketchup
1 cup brown sugar
½ cup chopped onion
1 tablespoon liquid smoke
½ teaspoon garlic powder

Combine Sauce ingredients and pour over meatballs. Bake at 350° for 1 hour.

Deer's Leap Winery

1520 Harpersfield Road • Geneva, OH 44041
440-466-1248 • www.deersleapwine.com

Deer's Leap Winery offers a casual atmosphere with a covered deck and spacious showroom. The Winery boast a variety of wine from sweet Fredonia to a dry Cabernet, as well as a vast selection of fruit wine. International award winning wine maker Robert Bostwick welcomes guests to enjoy the wines perfected by his 35 years of experience. Snacks are available in addition to a full kitchen serving lunch and dinner. Open all year round, Deer's Leap Winery is conveniently located off I-90 at exit 218 approximately 0.2 mile south on OH-534. Stop by and experience the tradition of fine wine.

Grecian Meatballs
(Keftedes)

2 slices white bread
1 pound ground chuck
1 egg
1 medium onion, chopped fine
½ tablespoon oregano
½ tablespoon fresh parsley
½ tablespoon mint
2 tablespoons olive oil
3 cloves garlic
2 tablespoons butter
Salt and pepper to taste
Flour
¾ cup seasoned breadcrumbs

Trim and discard crust from bread. Place bread in mixing bowl and moisten with a small amount of water. Gently squeeze bread to drain excess water. Add meat, egg, onion, oregano, garlic, mint, salt, pepper and parsley. Mix well with your hands. Shape into tiny balls about 1-inch thick.

For fried keftedes, coat with flour, heat butter and oil in a heavy skillet and fry meatballs over medium heat, turning 1 at a time. Drain on paper towels.

For baked keftedes, place meatballs in single layer on a baking sheet and bake at 350° for 15 minutes. Makes 36 small meatballs.

Taverna Committee
Holy Trinity Greek Food Festival
Historic Fort Steuben

Lasagna

2 pounds ground beef
1 pound hot breakfast sausage
3 cloves garlic, finely chopped
1 (28-ounce) can diced tomatoes, undrained
1 (6-ounce) can tomato paste
Salt and freshly ground pepper to taste
1 tablespoon olive oil
10 ounces lasagna noodles
1 pound mozzarella
10 to 12 fresh basil leaves
¼ cup fresh flat-leaf parsley leaves
3 cups low-fat cottage cheese
1 cup freshly grated Parmesan cheese
2 eggs, beaten

Preheat oven to 350°. In a large skillet over medium-high heat, sauté ground beef, sausage and garlic until brown; drain. Add tomatoes, tomato paste, salt and pepper. Stir together well. Simmer over low heat, uncovered, for 45 minutes stirring occasionally. Bring a large pot of water to a boil. Add olive oil and a dash of salt. Cook lasagna noodles according to package directions until al dente. Drain noodles and lay them flat on a piece of aluminum foil to keep their shape. Grate mozzarella cheese and set aside. Finely cut basil and parsley. Add half of the herbs to meat mixture and stir together.

In a medium bowl, combine remaining herbs, cottage cheese, half the Parmesan and eggs. Stir together well. Lay 4 lasagna noodles in bottom of a greased 9x13-inch baking dish. Noodles should overlap. Spoon half cottage cheese mixture onto noodles; spread evenly. Sprinkle half of mozzarella on top of cottage cheese mixture. Spoon just under half of meat mixture on top of mozzarella and spread evenly, being careful not to disturb layers below. Repeat, ending with a thick layer of meat sauce. Sprinkle remaining Parmesan on top. Bake until hot and bubbly, 35 to 45 minutes. Stand 10 minutes before cutting .

Union County Covered Bridge Bluegrass Festival

Hobo Dinner

Nonstick aluminum foil
1½ pounds ground beef
6 red potatoes, peeled and cubed
2½ cups carrots, diced large
1½ yellow onions, diced large
Salt and pepper to taste
Shredded Cheddar cheese
Condiments if desired: Ketchup, Worcestershire sauce, Barbeque sauce

Cut 6 (12x12-inch) pieces of aluminum foil. Be sure to spray foil with cooking spray unless using nonstick foil. Separate ground beef into 6 patties and place in center of foil (1 patty per piece of foil). Divide red potatoes, carrots and yellow onion evenly between dinners and place on top of meat. Sprinkle with salt and pepper. Fold up foil tightly around each meal. Double wrap if the foil is not big enough. Cook on grill on medium-high heat or over an open fire for 25 to 30 minutes—until vegetables and meat are cooked through. Open foil carefully, then top with cheese and condiments as desired.

Ozone Zipline Adventures

Ozone Zipline Adventures

YMCA Camp Kern

5291 State Route 350 • Oregonia, OH 45054

513-932-3756 • www.ozonezips.org

Since opening in 2009, Ozone Zipline Adventures has given more than 40,000 guests the experience of a lifetime, zipping through the beautiful Little Miami River Valley. Ozone boasts a hands-free braking course led by fun and professional tour guides who handle all safety measures and procedures. Guests will encounter breathtaking mile-long views of the Little Miami River. Tours start at $65 per person with special discounts available. There are 3 tour options: The Traditional Tour with 7 ziplines, River Tour with 9 ziplines, and Ultimate Tour with 11 ziplines. Ozone Zipline Adventures also offers a Night Zip Tour 1 weekend per month for $55 per person. Guests will experience the forest at night by the light of the full moon. Gift Certificates and Season Passes are available year-round.

Italian Beef

3- to 5-pound sirloin tip roast
1 (16-ounce) jar pepperoncini peppers
Juice of ½ lemon
2 tablespoons fresh minced garlic
1 tablespoon oregano
1 tablespoon basil
1 tablespoon parsley
1 (24-ounce) jar Newman's Own Marinara Sauce
Shredded mozzarella cheese

Place roast in slow cooker. Add pepperoncini peppers with their juice (reserving a few peppers for garnish), lemon juice and all spices. Add water until contents of slow cooker are covered. Cook on low 6 to 8 hours. Remove beef and shred. Place shredded beef back in slow cooker and cook on low another half hour. Serve beef over bread of your choice. Top with pepperoncini peppers, marinara sauce and shredded mozzarella cheese.

Hocking Hills Tourism Association

Herb Stuffed Pork Chops

¾ cup finely chopped onion
¼ cup finely chopped celery
2 tablespoons butter
2 cups coarse dry breadcrumbs
½ cup fresh parsley, minced
⅓ cup evaporated milk
¼ teaspoon salt
⅛ teaspoon pepper
10 large pork chops, cut with pockets
1 to 2 tablespoons vegetable oil
¾ cup clear chicken broth

In a large skillet, sauté onion and celery in butter until tender and slightly browned. Remove from heat. Pour in a bowl; add breadcrumbs, parsley, milk, salt and pepper. Toss to coat. Spoon about ¼ cup stuffing mixture into pockets of chops. In skillet, brown chops in oil. Sprinkle with salt and pepper.

Transfer browned chops to a baking pan sprayed with nonstick cooking spray. Pour chicken broth over chops and cover pan. Bake at 350° for 1 to 1½ hours, until very tender and moist. Spoon broth over chops before serving.

Twin Creek Tea Room
19 East Dayton Street • West Alexandria, OH 45381

Flank Steak

¼ cup olive oil
2 tablespoons soy sauce
2 tablespoons lemon juice
1 teaspoon celery salt
1 teaspoon coarse ground pepper
2 smashed garlic cloves
1 to 2 pounds flank steak

Mix together and pour into plastic bag with flank steak. Marinate at least 2 hours. Cook over charcoal grill.

Bonnybrook Farms

Lantern Light Wagon Rides & Corn Maze

Fun on the Farm, Homemade Dinner, Wagon Ride & Corn Maze

Saturday evenings in October
Reservations not required – Rides leave continually

Bonnybrook Farms
3779 State Route 132 • Clarksville, OH 45113
937-289-2500 • www.BonnybrookFarms.com

A Lantern Light Wagon Ride is a family-friendly, history-based ghost tour. After dark, board the wagon for a 40 minute lantern lit ride along the old stone roads of Bonnybrook Farms...back to a time when only lanterns lit the way. Follow the tracks of the "Old Sheepskin" railway...traverse the great hunting ground of the Shawnee Indians along Todd Fork Creek...and peer through the ruins of what used to be. Catch a glimpse of travelers past! Wagon riders meet trappers, Indians, frontiersmen and pioneer settlers portrayed by professional theater actors along the way. Afterward return to the Gathering Barn for s'mores around the campfire.

Shiitake Fettuccine with Sweet Chile-Soy Pork & Sausage

1 (12-ounce) pork tenderloin
¼ cup soy sauce
¼ cup sweet chili sauce
2 cups asparagus, trimmed and cut into 1-inch lengths
1 tablespoon sesame oil
½ cup chicken stock
1 (12-ounce) package Rossi Pasta Shiitake Fettuccine
1 tablespoon sesame seeds, toasted
2 tablespoons green onions, chopped

Place pork tenderloin in 1-gallon zip-close bag, add soy sauce and sweet chili sauce. Seal and shake. Allow to marinate for at least 2 hours. Prepare grill and grill tenderloin till medium-done. Reserve the marinade. Allow to rest 5 minutes before slicing. In large sauté pan, sauté asparagus in sesame oil 3 minutes over medium heat. Add stock and reserved marinade, bring to boil. Simmer 3 to 5 minutes. Cook pasta according to package directions. Toss pasta with asparagus mixture. Slice pork and arrange on top of pasta. Garnish with sesame seeds and green onions.

Rossi Pasta
106 Front Street, Marietta OH 45750

Marietta-Washington County Convention and Visitors Bureau

119 Greene Street • Marietta, OH 45750
740-373-5178 • www.mariettaohio.org

Enjoy historically fascinating Bold Beginnings and experience adrenaline pumping New Adventures in Marietta-Washington County. Rich with history, outdoor recreation, a lively downtown and delicious dining opportunities, it's one of the premier getaway destinations in the state. Food and beverage enthusiasts have plenty to explore with options ranging from the eclectic, fine cuisine of The Buckley House Restaurant, the brew pub atmosphere of the Marietta Brewing Company, a mom and pop feel at The Original Pizza Place and so much more.

Here's what the experts are saying about Marietta-Washington County:

"Ohio's Best Adventure Town"—*National Geographic*

"One of the Top 20 Best Small Towns to Visit"—*Smithsonian Magazine*

"One of Ohio's Best Hometowns"—*Ohio Magazine*

"One of the most Beautiful Small Towns in America"—*Impulicty*

Broccoli Chicken Divan

1 large bunch fresh broccoli, cut apart
2 cups shredded Cheddar cheese, divided
1 (8-ounce) can sliced water chestnuts, drained
½ cup chopped onion
4 cups cooked chicken breast, cut into 1-inch-wide strips
1 cup mayonnaise
2 (10¾-ounce) cans cream of chicken soup
1 tablespoon lemon juice
1 tablespoon Worcestershire sauce
½ cup dry breadcrumbs
3 tablespoons butter, finely chopped

Cook broccoli just until crisp and tender; drain. Arrange in a greased 9x13-inch baking dish. Sprinkle 1 cup cheese, water chestnuts and onion over broccoli. Next, layer cooked chicken breast strips. In medium bowl, combine mayonnaise, soup, lemon juice and Worcestershire sauce. Spread over chicken. Top with remaining cheese. In separate bowl, combine breadcrumbs and chopped butter; mix well. Spread breadcrumb mixture over cheese. Bake at 350° for 30 to 45 minutes or until bubbly. Serve immediately.

Recipe courtesy of Twin Creek Tea Room
19 East Dayton Street, West Alexandria, OH 45381
Preble County Convention & Visitors Bureau

Preble County Pork Festival

Third Full Weekend in September

Preble County Fairgrounds

722 South Franklin Street • Eaton, OH 45320

937-456-7273 • www.porkfestival.org

Little did those who planned the first Preble County Pork Festival in 1971 envision their efforts would lead to a phenomenon that has grown from selling ham sandwiches out of plastic foam coolers to an Expo Center and midway filled with vendors and entertainment for tens of thousands festival-goers. There is free parking, free admission and great food. There is fresh grilled pork chops, ham, pulled pork and smoked sausage sandwiches, and terrific pulled pork nachos, all-you-can-eat pancake and sausage breakfast, and then a lunch and supper pork chop smorgasbord! Within three days, over 50,000 pork chops are fresh cut for the grills and Country Store. There are exhibitors from all over the US for a truly marvelous shopping experience. The weather is usually beautiful because the third weekend in September is statistically the driest weekend in Eaton!

Cynthia's Lemon Chicken

1 pound boneless, skinless chicken breasts, cut into strips
1 egg
1 sleeve saltine crackers, crushed
Butter
Lemon juice

Preheat oven to 350°. Roll each piece of chicken strip in beaten egg and then coat with cracker crumbs. Brown chicken strips in frying pan with butter and lemon juice. Place chicken strips in baking dish with lemon and butter from frying pan. Add extra lemon and butter to baking dish to taste. Bake 25 minutes.

Robbie Jenkins
Gallipolis River Recreational Festival

Gallipolis River Recreational Festival

July

Gallipolis City Park • Gallipolis, OH 45631
740-446-0596 • www.gallipolisriverrec.com

Located in picturesque downtown Gallipolis' City Park, the annual Gallipolis River Recreation Festival is Gallia County's main event for the July 4th holiday. Organized by the Gallia County Chamber of Commerce, in partnership with the City of Gallipolis and area businesses, the multiple day event features numerous activities ranging from live entertainment to a Kids Day with old fashioned games, such as watermelon eating and sack races, concluding with a fireworks display over the Ohio River. While visiting the Festival, guests can also take a stroll along the streets of historic downtown Gallipolis and visit the many shops in the area.

Chicken Linguine with Spicy Pesto

2 tablespoons olive oil
1 pound boneless, skinless chicken breasts, cut into ⅓-inch strips
Beau Monde seasoning
Black pepper to taste
1 leek, sliced
⅓ cup fresh cilantro, chopped
⅓ cup chopped pecans, toasted
1 tablespoon roasted garlic, minced
2 teaspoons seeded jalapeños, minced (add seeds to increase spiciness)
¼ teaspoon dried, crushed red pepper
½ cup basil pesto
12 ounces linguine
Additional cilantro, chopped
Fresh Parmesan cheese, shaved

Heat olive oil in heavy, large skillet over medium-high heat. Season chicken with Beau Monde and black pepper. Add chicken to skillet and sauté until cooked through and beginning to brown, 3 to 4 minutes. Using slotted spoon, transfer chicken into bowl. Add leek, cilantro, pecans, garlic, jalapeño and dried red pepper to same skillet. Sauté until leeks wilt, about 5 minutes. Add pesto, chicken and any accumulated juices. Stir to blend. Remove from heat. Meanwhile, cook linguine in large pot of salted water al dente. Drain, reserving ⅓ cup cooking liquid. Bring sauce to simmer. Add linguine and reserved cooking liquid and toss to coat. Season to taste with salt and pepper. Top with additional cilantro and shaved Parmesan.

Welsh Hills Inn

Yuletide Chicken

This five-ingredient main dish, which looks like a holiday present on rice, will wow guests.

4 (5-ounce) skinless, boneless chicken breast halves
Freshly ground pepper
1 (5-ounce) container cream cheese (French onion, garlic and herb, or garden vegetable flavor)
8 sheets frozen phyllo dough, thawed
⅓ cup butter, melted
Hot cooked rice

Rinse chicken; pat dry with paper towels. Place each chicken breast half between 2 pieces of plastic wrap and pound lightly until about ¼-inch thick. Sprinkle with pepper. Place approximately 1½ tablespoons cheese in center of each piece of chicken. Fold in sides and roll chicken up, jelly-roll style.

Line a baking sheet with parchment paper or foil. Evenly stack 8 phyllo dough sheets on a work surface. With a sharp knife, cut phyllo stack into 12-inch squares; discard trimmings. Generously brush 1 square with butter. Place another square on top; brush with butter. Keep repeating until all 8 sheets are coated. Place a chicken breast, seam side down, on phyllo stack. Gather up 2 sheets of phyllo to form a bundle, twisting top slightly to hold it together. With a spatula, transfer to prepared baking sheet. Repeat with remaining phyllo squares and chicken breasts. Bake at 375° for 25 to 30 minutes or until phyllo is golden. Serve baked chicken package on top of a serving of hot cooked rice.

The Barn Inn Bed and Breakfast

Chicken Enchiladas

2 cups cooked chicken, cut up or shredded
2 cups sour cream
2 (4-ounce) cans mild diced green chiles
½ cup chopped green onion
½ teaspoon salt
4 cups shredded Jack cheese
12 flour tortillas
1 (16-ounce) can mild enchilada sauce

Preheat oven to 375°. Combine chicken, sour cream, green chiles, onion, salt and cheese; mix well. Grease bottom of 9x13-inch baking dish. Dip 1 side of tortillas in enchilada sauce and place ⅔ cup filling down middle. Roll tortilla and place side by side in pan. Top with leftover sauce and cheese. Bake uncovered 20 to 30 minutes.

Pine Lakes Lodge Bed & Breakfast

Pine Lakes Lodge Bed & Breakfast

61680 Buskirk Lane • Salesville, OH 43778
740-679-3617 • www.pinelakeslodge.com

Nestled in the beautiful, forested hills of southeastern Ohio, Pine Lakes Lodge stands out among other Ohio bed and breakfast establishments by placing our focus on each guest. At Pine Lakes Lodge, guests will be delighted to discover all of the creature comforts, and they will find friendly people waiting to greet and assist. Whether looking for the ideal place to hold a corporate retreat, family reunion, or wedding, or to escape for a romantic weekend getaway, Pine Lakes Lodge is the choice destination for unsurpassed beauty and unparalleled service.

Chicken Cutlets

2 cups plain breadcrumbs
1 cup Romano cheese, grated
Fresh parsley, finely chopped
2 cloves garlic, minced
2 or 3 boneless chicken breasts
1 or 2 eggs, lightly beaten

Combine breadcrumbs, cheese, parsley and garlic. Use fingers to incorporate garlic throughout ingredients. Place 1 of the chicken breasts between 2 pieces of plastic wrap and pound with meat mallet until thin. Continue with remaining breasts. They may be cut if the pieces are too large. Dip chicken, 1 at a time, in the beaten egg and then in the breadcrumb mixture. Heat olive oil in skillet and fry cutlets until golden brown. Drain thoroughly on paper towels before serving.

Susan Trivison Klug
Laurello Vineyards

Laurello Vineyards

4573 State Route 307 East
Geneva, OH 44010
440-415-0661
www.laurellovineyards.com

Laurello Vineyards is a boutique winery nestled in the Grand River Valley of Geneva, Ohio. The winery is a place for old friends to gather and new friends to meet in a relaxed, cordial atmosphere. The Winery strives to provide hand-crafted wines, paired with homemade foods that enhance the flavors of the wines. Most importantly, they will educate, satisfy and always make guests feel at home.

Stuffed Chicken Filled with Love!

½ pound spinach, trimmed and washed
4 tablespoons olive oil, divided, for cooking
1½ pounds dry goat cheese, crumbled
3 garlic cloves, minced
5 green onions, minced
2 black bell peppers, minced
3 tablespoons fresh sage, rolled and sliced thin
3 tablespoons fresh parsley, minced
Salt and pepper to taste
2 (8-ounce) chicken breasts, cut ¼-inch thick
Kale or other leafy green for plate garnish

Sauté spinach in 2 tablespoons olive oil over medium-high heat till wilted. Set aside. When cooled slightly, mix with remaining filling ingredients in a large mixing bowl. Season with salt and pepper. Place 1 to 2 tablespoons of filling at the edge of a cutlet, lengthwise. Evenly roll chicken till other side touches to seal. Repeat till all chicken is rolled, or filling is used. Tie chicken with butcher's twine at each end and once in the center. Heat a skillet with 2 tablespoons olive oil over medium-high heat. When simmering, lay chicken in pan, seam side down. Cook 2 to 3 minutes, rolling to all sides, till internal temperature reaches 165°. Remove and place on paper towel. Let rest 2 to 3 minutes before slicing. Slice on an angle into bite-size rings. Serve over a bed of kale or other leafy greens.

Chef Patrick Nipper and Chef Steve "Soupy" Townsend
Oxford Kinetics Festival

Raspberry Glazed Chicken

½ cup Cooper's Mill Seedless Raspberry Jam
1 tablespoon Dijon mustard
6 boneless, skinless chicken breasts, halved (about 1¾ pounds)

Brush grill with vegetable oil or prepare nonstick frying pan. Mix together Cooper's Mill Raspberry Jam and Dijon mustard. Place chicken on grill or in pan and cover. Cook on medium heat 20 to 25 minutes, brushing occasionally with jam mixture. Turn chicken halfway into cooking. Remove from heat and check that the chicken is cooked through. Discard remaining jam mixture.

Note: Try using Cooper's Mill Raspberry Jalapeño Jam for a spicier version.

Cooper's Mill Apple Butter & Jelly Factory

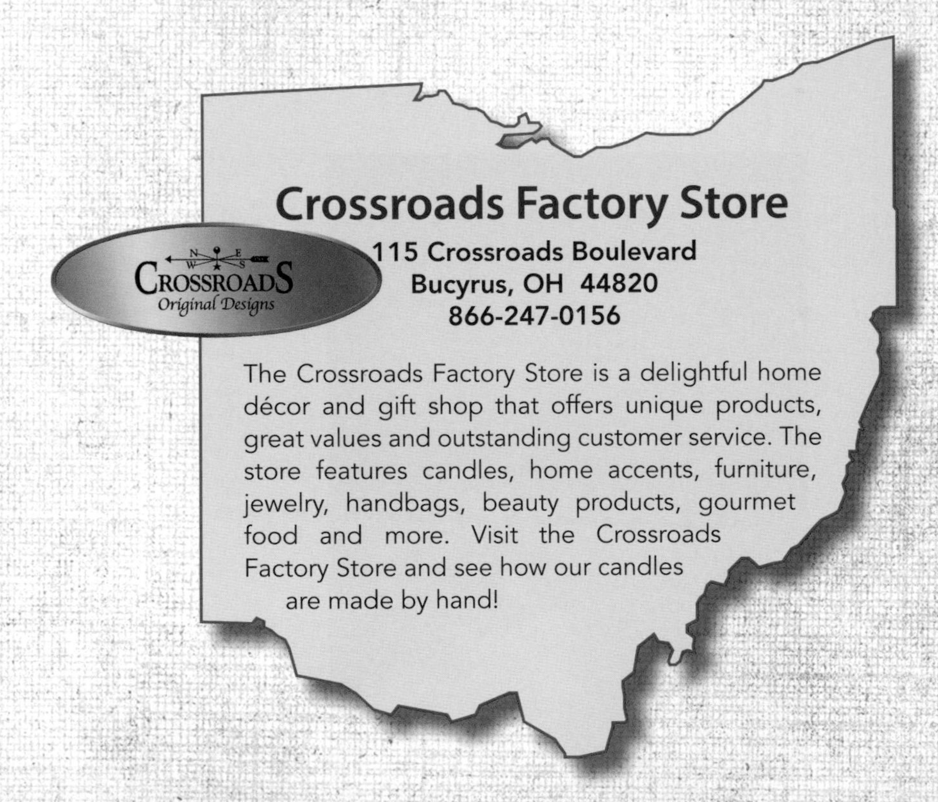

Stuffed Green Peppers

6 large green bell peppers
1 pound ground turkey
1½ cups cooked rice
⅓ cup chopped onion
1 (4-ounce) can mushrooms
1 teaspoon salt
⅛ teaspoon pepper
1 (28-ounce) can spicy spaghetti sauce
¼ cup sugar

Wash peppers, and cut off tops and remove seeds and ribs; parboil in covered pan with ½-inch water. Set aside when done.

Combine turkey with rice, onion, mushrooms, salt and pepper. In separate bowl, combine spaghetti sauce and sugar. Blend all but ¼ cup into meat and rice mixture. Stuff peppers and place upright in baking pan. Pour remaining ¼ cup sauce over peppers, cover and bake at 350° for 45 minutes and then 15 minutes uncovered.

Bonnybrook Farms

Chuck Wagon Dinner Rides

Fun on the Farm, Homemade Dinner & Wagon Ride

Saturdays in June, July, August & September
5:00pm to 9:00pm • Reservations required
Weekday and weekend dates available for private groups

Bonnybrook Farms
3779 State Route 132 • Clarksville, OH 45113
937-289-2500 • www.BonnybrookFarms.com

A chuck wagon dinner ride offers a fun evening of great food and camaraderie for families, friends and groups of all sizes on a beautiful and historic 370-acre working farm. Work up a hearty appetite before dinner with some "fun on the farm" activities like clodhopper golf, giant slingshots, corn hole, horseshoe hill with an 80-foot underground slide, friendly farm animals, feed the big fish, farmyard play area, and a catch and release fishing pond. When the dinner bell rings, enjoy a delicious "made from scratch" dinner of hickory smoked pork and chicken, Nathan's hot dogs and fresh locally grown salads and sides. Dine in the post and beam gathering barn or on the back porch overlooking the farm pond. After dinner, board the wagon for a ride down an abandoned country road to the old Chuck Wagon at Todd Fork Creek for homemade desserts and s'mores around a campfire.

Spaghetti Squash with Ground Turkey and Tomato Sauce

1 medium spaghetti squash (about 4 pounds), rinsed well
3 tablespoons extra virgin olive oil, divided
2 cups diced sweet onion
12 white button mushrooms, stemmed, then sliced (about 2 cups)
1 cup frozen peas, optional
1 medium zucchini, diced, optional
Salt and pepper to taste
1 (14.5-ounce) can diced Italian-style tomatoes (preferably no salt added), plus their juices
½ cup dry white wine
2 cloves garlic, pressed or minced
1 pound 95% lean, ground white turkey meat or ground chicken breast
Freshly grated Parmigiano-Reggiano cheese for garnish, optional

Preheat oven to 350°. Cut squash lengthwise in half, avoiding the stem. Place halves, cut sides up, in a baking dish. Bake 45 minutes or until flesh is easily pierced with a knife. Cool completely. Meanwhile, heat 2 tablespoons oil in a large sauté pan over medium heat. Once oil simmers, add onion, mushrooms, peas, zucchini, salt and pepper, stirring to coat. Cook 10 minutes, stirring occasionally.

Stir in tomatoes and their juices, wine and garlic; cover and cook 10 minutes to create a chunky sauce, breaking up the tomatoes as they cook. Heat remaining tablespoon of oil in a separate medium skillet over medium heat. Once oil simmers, add meat. Season with salt and pepper. Cook 15 minutes, using a wooden spoon to break up clumps. The meat should be completely browned. Add meat to sauce until well-incorporated and heated through; set aside till squash is prepared. Scoop out squash seeds. Use a fork (or 2) to shred squash flesh, dragging fork through lengthwise. Transfer strands to a mixing bowl or serving platter. Discard the empty skins. Spoon sauce over squash and toss well. Garnish with cheese, if desired. Serve right away.

Knox County Convention & Visitors Bureau

Sweet and Spicy Apple Butter Chipotle Chicken Thighs

10 garlic cloves, minced
1 medium yellow onion, chopped
3 to 5 chipotles in adobo sauce, chopped
¼ cup Worcestershire sauce
¾ cup apple butter
8 chicken thighs

Combine garlic, onion, chipotles, Worcestershire and apple butter in a dish and mix. Place chicken thighs in a plastic bag and add marinade; rub together until fully covered. Refrigerate at least 3 hours. Preheat oven to 425°. Line a 9x13-inch baking dish with foil, spray with cooking spray. Place thighs skin up in dish and cover with marinade. Bake 30 to 45 minutes or until the internal temperature is 165°. Rest 5 minutes before serving.

Grand Rapids Applebutter Fest

Lamb Shanks

4 lamb shanks
1 tomato, chopped
½ onion, chopped
2 garlic cloves
1 stalk celery, chopped
1 carrot, chopped
1 sprig rosemary
1 cup red wine
4 quarts beef stock
1 tablespoon melted butter
1 tablespoon flour plus more for dusting

Preheat oven to 325°. Place all ingredients, except butter and flour, into a deep pan. Bake 4 hours. Check meat with a fork to see if the meat pulls away from the bone and is tender. Remove shanks from liquid and set aside. Strain vegetables from liquid and discard, reserving liquid. Make a roux with 1 tablespoon melted butter and 1 tablespoon flour in saucepan. Whisk together until smooth. Whisk in reserved liquid till smooth. Simmer roughly 20 minutes until sauce thickens. Heat 2 tablespoons oil in a large pan over medium heat. Dust shanks with flour, add to pan and brown on both sides. Serve lamb with sauce.

Canal Tavern of Zoar

The Lamb Burger

The General Denver Hotel prides itself in including local products on their menu, and the Lamb Burger is no exception. They use locally sourced lamb from the Taylor's Tunis in Sabina, Ohio. Taylor's Tunis is a small, family run farm owned by Bruce and Debbie Linebaugh who raise the Tunis breed of lamb, known for its red points and usefulness as a meat and for wool production. The Lamb Burger is one of their most delicious and popular selections. The ground lamb is prepared with feta cheese, roasted red peppers and herbs making the meat even more flavorful, tender and delicious. The lamb is topped with a hand-breaded fried green tomato and fresh mozzarella cheese. Situated on homemade Ciabatta bread, arugula and house-prepared remoulade garnish the burger with a peppery, tangy flair.

The General Denver Hotel
81 West Main Street • Wilmington, OH 45177
937-383-4141

EXPLORE

Clinton County, OH 45177

What is sometimes overlooked as an alternative destination is the rural community of Clinton County. Slightly off the beaten path, Clinton County has treasures of its own to offer, away from the hustle and bustle of the large city. The ambiance of rural America is not a myth, it is as real as the people who reside there, who cherish old fashioned values, who are neighborly, and who know what it is to be hospitable. The people who travel rural America are looking for something special. Clinton County visitors will find historic relics, architecture, and art, museums without huge, loud crowds, shops with antiques, and quiet, delicious dinners. There are festivals where family is still the focal point, and a community that respects the opportunity to create their own memories. Clinton County represents the epitome of rural America.

Rosemary Citrus Lamb Shoulder

Pairs well with Maqui, Via Vecchia's Chilean Malbec.

1 teaspoon extra virgin olive oil
2 (8- to 12-ounce) lamb shoulders
¼ ounce fresh rosemary, about 4 large sprigs
1 clementine orange
¼ teaspoon Himalayan pink sea salt

In a skillet (cast iron for best results) on medium heat, add olive oil then lamb shoulders and cook, covered, for 8 minutes. Flip lamb shoulders and cook another 8 minutes, or until meat begins to turn grey and a slight smoke rises. Once lamb shoulders are grey on both sides, add 2 rosemary sprigs on top of each shoulder. Zest the clementine and sprinkle the zest and sea salt over both pieces, to desired amount. Cover for about 6 minutes, then carefully press rosemary into lamb so that you can flip once more. After flipping lamb, rosemary face down, squeeze desired amount of juice from clementine to add a sweet, citrus flavor. Cook until meat darkens. Once pink is gone, or as rare as you prefer, serve!

Michael Elmer
Via Vecchia Winery

Roasted Lamb

The founders of The Olive Scene all have Mediterranean heritage, and their holiday meals reflect the culinary traditions of Italy, Greece, and Turkey. As a result, Easter celebrations would not be the same without a platter of herby, garlicky roasted lamb. This dish is amazing with roasted or mashed potatoes, roasted asparagus or a beautiful salad with a mustardy, lemony dressing.

6- to 7-pound bone-in leg of lamb or 5- to 6-pound boneless leg of lamb
8 cloves garlic, 4 sliced thinly and 4 chopped
Salt and pepper to taste
Juice from 1 lemon
1½ tablespoons chopped fresh rosemary
½ tablespoon dried Sicilian oregano (found at The Olive Scene), can substitute any dried oregano
2 tablespoons extra virgin olive oil (Any single varietal will work, but if you want even more flavor try rosemary flavor. Also good with Tuscan Herb, Garlic or Lemon olive oils.)

Preheat the oven to 400°. Cut small slits into skin of lamb and insert slices of garlic. Salt and pepper to taste. Combine chopped garlic, lemon juice, rosemary, oregano and olive oil in a small bowl. Spread liberally over outside of lamb. Place lamb in a roasting pan and roast 45 minutes. Reduce heat to 375° and cook another 45 to 60 minutes, until a thermometer registers 135° for medium-rare, 145° for medium or 155° for well-done. Tent with foil and allow meat to rest 15 minutes before carving.

The Olive Scene

Gina Maria Venison

The rich flavors of the Pinot Noir bring out the best in this game dinner, due to the spicy aftertones and truffle flavors which compliment the richness of the venison flavor.

1½ to 3 pounds venison round steak, cut into 1-inch cubes
¼ cup flour
¼ cup butter
½ cup chopped onion
1 tablespoon dried parsley
1 garlic clove, chopped
1 bay leaf
1 teaspoon salt
½ pound fresh mushrooms, sliced
1 cup Gina Maria Pinot Noir
½ cup water
Cooked rice

Toss meat cubes in flour and brown lightly in butter over medium heat. Add onion, parsley, garlic, bay leaf, salt and mushrooms. Cook until onion is just tender. Slowly add wine and water, stirring constantly. Bring just to boiling, reduce heat and simmer until the meat is tender. Add more wine if necessary. Remove bay leaf and serve over rice.

Powell Village Winery & Tasting Room

Powell Village Winery & Tasting Room

50 South Liberty Street, Suite 174 • Powell, OH 43065
614-505-7465
www.PowellVillageWinery.com
www.facebook.com/PowellVillageWinery

Tuesday through Thursday: 3pm to 9pm
Friday: 3pm to 10pm • Saturday: 12pm to 10pm
CLOSED Sunday and Monday

As an artisan wine producer, the Powell Village Winery sources, blends and produces small lots of high quality vinifera wines from America's notable grape-growing regions. From bold and dry to sweet and fruity, they strive to create a diverse range of distinct wines for every taste. They have followed in the footsteps of micro breweries and have brought the grapes to the people, locally handcrafting all of their wines right in Powell, Ohio. Please stop by and visit their award winning tasting room located in beautiful downtown historic Powell, a suburb of Columbus, Ohio.

Smoked Trout Pasta

8 ounces angel hair pasta
3 tablespoons butter
1 tablespoon minced onion
1 tablespoon minced garlic
1 red bell pepper, diced
1 carrot, julienne sliced
1 cup asparagus, bite-size pieces
⅔ cup heavy cream
½ cup grated Parmesan
Salt and pepper to taste
1 pound smoked trout fillets, skinned and diced
¼ teaspoon ground nutmeg, optional

Cook pasta according to package directions. Heat butter in hot skillet with onion and garlic. Sauté bell pepper, carrot and asparagus until just beginning to be tender. Stir in cream and bring to a boil. Reduce heat and stir in Parmesan cheese, salt and pepper. Simmer until sauce thickens. Just before serving, toss pasta with sauce and diced smoked trout. Garnish with nutmeg.

The FoodSmiths Catering
Freshwater Farms of Ohio

Freshwater Farms of Ohio

2624 North US Highway 68 • Urbana, OH 43078
937-652-3701 • 800-634-7434
www.fwfarms.com

Visit year round, Monday through Saturday, 10am to 6pm

Freshwater Farms is Ohio's largest indoor fish hatchery. Their specialties are hand-cut boneless fillets and smoked trout fillets and spreads, seasoned trout patties, marinated and pre-seasoned fillets. All products are made with all natural ingredients and contain no artificial preservatives. Other Ohio products, including cheeses, honey, maple syrup, and potato chips are available. The farm is open to the public for free, self-guided tours where guests can view live exhibits, feed trout by hand and pet rare, endangered sturgeon at the sturgeon petting zoo. Guided tours of the fish farm require advanced registration and a small fee, and can include a gourmet sampling of all-natural smoked trout spreads. Also available are stocking fish, pond fountains, water garden plants and virtually anything needed for ponds or water gardens.

Poached Salmon with Irish Butter Sauce

2 pounds center-cut fresh salmon
Salt (1 tablespoon salt per 2 pints water)

Irish Butter Sauce:
2 egg yolks
2 teaspoons cold water
1 stick butter, diced
1 teaspoon lemon juice
Flat-leaf parsley, fennel leaves and lemon wedges for garnish

Choose a saucepan that will barely fit the piece of fish: an oval saucepan is perfect. (It is important to use the smallest saucepan possible.) Half fill saucepan with salted water and bring to a boil. Put in piece of fish, bring back to a boil, cover and simmer very gently 20 minutes.

Turn off heat and allow fish to sit in water while making the sauce (do not let sit for more than 20 minutes). Put egg yolks in a heavy stainless steel saucepan on low heat or in a bowl over hot water (double boiler). Add water and whisk thoroughly. Add butter, bit by bit, whisking constantly. As soon as 1 piece melts, add the next. Mixture will gradually thicken, but if it shows signs of becoming too thick or slightly scrambling, remove from heat immediately and add a little cold water. Do not leave pan or stop whisking until sauce is made. If sauce is too slow to thicken it may be because you are excessively cautious and the heat is too low. Increase heat slightly and continue to whisk until the sauce thickens to a coating consistency. Add lemon juice. Just before serving, skin salmon and lay it on a hot serving dish. Garnish with parsley, fennel leaves and lemon wedges and serve with the Irish Butter Sauce.

Fitzgerald's Irish Bed & Breakfast

Desserts & Other Sweets

Spiced Pear & Apple Pie

- 1 Classic **Crisco®** Pie Crust (see page 192)
- 4 cups peeled, thinly sliced pears
- 2 cups peeled, thinly sliced apples
- ¾ cup sugar
- 2 tablespoons Pillsbury BEST™ All Purpose Flour
- ¾ teaspoon ground cinnamon
- ¼ teaspoon ground ginger
- ¼ teaspoon salt
- 1 tablespoon lemon juice
- Milk
- Cinnamon sugar

Prepare recipe for double crust pie. Roll out dough for bottom crust. Place in 9-inch pie plate. Press to fit without stretching dough. Trim even with pie plate. Preheat oven to 400°. Combine pears, apples, sugar, flour, cinnamon, ginger, salt and lemon juice in large bowl. Spoon into prepared pie crust. Roll out dough for top crust. Place onto filled pie or cut into strips creating a lattice top. Trim ½ inch beyond edge. Fold under bottom crust edge to seal. Crimp and flute edges. Cut slits in top crust or prick with fork to allow steam to escape. Brush crust with milk and sprinkle with cinnamon sugar. Bake 30 to 40 minutes or until apples are tender and crust is golden brown.

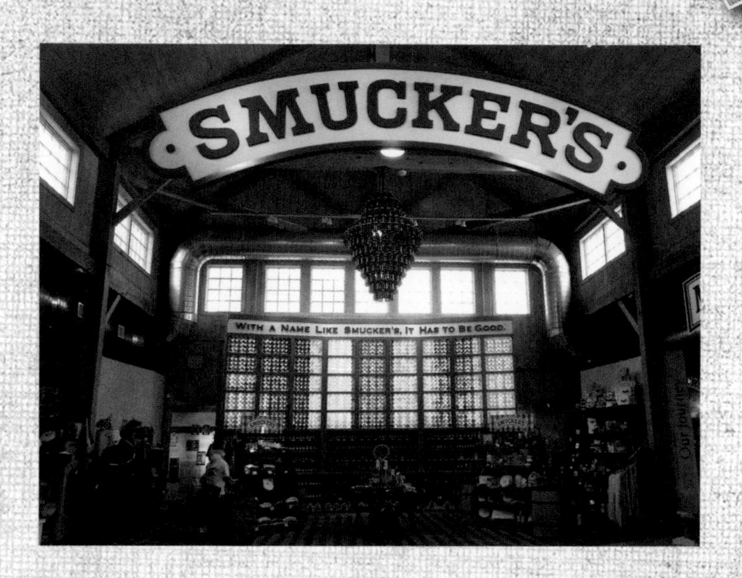

The J.M. Smucker Company Store and Cafe

333 Wadsworth Road • Orrville, OH 44667
330-684-1500

The J.M. Smucker Company was founded in 1897 in the town of Orrville when the Company's namesake and founder sold his first product—apple butter—from the back of a horse-drawn wagon. Since that time, the Company's trusted brands and quality ingredients have helped to make family meal time special.

Today, over a century later, the Company's broad range of products are featured at The J.M. Smucker Company Store and Cafe—the Company's showcase store.

Enjoy a create-your-own sundae in the Cafe and learn about the Company's humble beginnings in a walk-through museum. Unique recipe sampling and the custom gift basket design center are favorites among the many guests that visit each year.

Located at the entrance of Amish Country, the unique barn design adds to the scenic country view and has served as a must see tourist destination for Northeast Ohio.

Classic Crisco® Pie Crust

Double Crust for Spiced Pear & Apple Pie Recipe:
2 cups Pillsbury BEST™ All Purpose Flour
1 teaspoon salt
¾ stick well-chilled Crisco Baking Sticks All-Vegetable Shortening
OR ¾ cup well-chilled Crisco All-Vegetable Shortening
4 to 8 tablespoons ice cold water

Blend flour and salt in large bowl. Cut shortening into flour mixture using pastry blender or fork. Stir in just enough water with fork until dough holds together.

TIP: Test dough for proper moistness by squeezing a marble-sized ball of dough in your hand. If it holds together firmly, do not add any additional water. If the dough crumbles, add more water by the tablespoonful, until dough is moist enough to form a smooth ball when pressed together.

Divide dough in half; shape into balls. Flatten ball(s) into ½-inch thick round disk(s). Roll and bake according to specific recipe directions on page 190.

TIP: For ease in rolling, wrap dough in plastic wrap. Chill for 30 minutes or up to 2 days.

Creamy Peach Pie

1 (9-inch) unbaked pastry shell
¾ cups sugar
¼ cup flour
¼ teaspoon salt
¼ teaspoon nutmeg
3 cups peeled, sliced peaches
1 cup whipping cream

Mix sugar, flour, salt and nutmeg. Add peaches and toss lightly. Turn into pastry shell. Pour whipping cream over top of peaches. Bake at 400° for 35 to 45 minutes.

Apple Hill Orchards

Rhubarb Pie

4 cups fresh or frozen rhubarb
1¼ cups sugar
½ teaspoon cinnamon
¼ cup instant tapioca
Fresh or frozen pie crust

Combine rhubarb, sugar, cinnamon and tapioca in bowl; mix well. Place bottom crust in pie pan and fill with rhubarb mixture. Cover with second crust and crimp edges. Bake at 400° for 30 to 40 minutes then turn oven down to 350°. When pie juices bubble and bubbles don't burst quickly, it's done. Cool before cutting.

Bonnybrook Farms

Adams County Travel & Visitors Bureau Chocolate Pie

16 ounces cream cheese, softened
2½ cups powdered sugar
3 (3.9-ounce) packages instant chocolate pudding mix
4 cups milk
1 (16-ounce) carton Cool Whip, plus more for topping, if desired
4 baked pie crusts

Mix cream cheese and powdered sugar. Combine chocolate pudding mix and milk; let set. Add chocolate pudding mixture to cream cheese mixture. Fold in Cool Whip. Pour into baked pie crust. Top with Cool Whip, if desired. Makes 4 pies.

From Mary Miller's kitchen at Millers Bakery & Furniture
Adams County Convention & Visitors Bureau

Chocolate Chip Cheesecake

1½ cups graham cracker crumbs
⅓ cup sugar
⅓ cup butter, melted
3 (8-ounce) packages cream cheese, softened
1 (14-ounce) can condensed milk
2 teaspoons vanilla extract
3 eggs
1 cup mini semisweet chocolate chips, plus additional to sprinkle on top

Preheat oven to 300°. Mix graham cracker crumbs, sugar and butter. Press into bottom and up sides of 9-inch springform pan. Set crust aside. Beat cream cheese until smooth. Gradually add condensed milk; beat well. Add vanilla and eggs; beat on medium speed until smooth. Fold in chocolate chips. Pour into prepared crust. Sprinkle top with additional chocolate chips, if desired. Bake 1 hour. Turn off oven (do not open oven door) and leave cheesecake in oven to cool for another hour. Remove from oven and cool completely. Refrigerate before removing sides of pan. Keep cake refrigerated until ready to serve.

Destination Hilliard

New York Cheesecake

This cheesecake has won Grand Champion at the Hardin County Fair and Best of Show in 2014 at the Allen County Fair.

Crust:

2 cups graham cracker crumbs
3 tablespoons sugar
1 stick butter, melted

Spray all sides of 10-inch springform pan with nonstick spray. Combine graham cracker crumbs, sugar and melted butter. Mix well and press into pan. Bake at 350° until set, approximately 10 minutes. After Crust has cooled, double wrap pan with heavy duty aluminum foil.

Filling:

2 (8-ounce) packages cream cheese, softened
1½ cups sugar
1 (16-ounce) carton small curd cottage cheese
4 large eggs, beaten
1 teaspoon vanilla
1 tablespoon lemon juice
2 tablespoons flour
3 tablespoons cornstarch
3 tablespoons butter, softened
1 (16-ounce) carton sour cream

Cube cream cheese and place in food processor. Add sugar and blend well. Add cottage cheese; mix until very smooth. Blend in beaten eggs, vanilla and lemon juice. Add flour and cornstarch and mix. Blend in butter. Pour mixture into a large bowl and stir in sour cream until smooth. Pour into springform pan with the previously baked crust. Place into a larger jellyroll pan. Fill jellyroll pan with water, just below edge of pan. Bake in preheated 350° oven for 75 to 90 minutes or until set (doesn't jiggle in the middle). Do not overbake. Remove from oven and let completely cool. Cover and refrigerate overnight or until chilled.

Run knife around edge of pan to loosen the cheesecake, then release pan. Take a large knife and run under Crust and transfer to a cake plate. Top with cherry, raspberry or strawberry topping, if desired.

Union County Covered Bridge Bluegrass Festival

Bun's Fudge Cake Recipe

2¾ cups plus 2 tablespoons cake flour
2 cups sugar
1¾ cups solid vegetable shortening
½ cup unsweetened Dutch-process cocoa, such as Droste
4 tablespoons plus 2 teaspoons powdered milk
2½ teaspoons baking powder
1 teaspoon baking soda
1½ teaspoons vanilla extract
1 teaspoon salt
1½ cups water, divided
6 egg whites, room temperature

Preheat oven to 350°. Lightly grease and flour 2 (9-inch) round cake pans. In a large mixer bowl, combine flour, sugar, shortening, cocoa, powdered milk, baking powder, baking soda, vanilla, salt and 1 cup water. Beat on low speed and gradually increase to speed to high, until smooth and light, about 4 minutes. Add egg whites and ½ cup water. Beat until very smooth and light in texture, about 4 minutes. Divide batter between pans and smooth tops. Bake in center of oven 30 to 35 minutes, until cakes are puffed and tester inserted comes out clean. Cool in pans 10 minutes. Invert onto wire rack; cool completely.

Fudge Frosting:

4 ounces unsweetened chocolate
2 tablespoons solid vegetable shortening
4 cups powdered sugar
¼ teaspoon salt
½ cup plus 2 tablespoons milk, divided
1 teaspoon vanilla extract

In top of a double boiler, combine chocolate and shortening; warm over low heat, stirring until smooth. Immediately remove from heat. In a large bowl, combine powdered sugar, salt, ½ cup milk and vanilla. Stir until smooth. Scrape melted chocolate into sugar mixture and beat with a spoon until well blended. Let frosting stand 1 minute to thicken. Beat in remaining 2 tablespoons milk until smooth. Spread frosting between cake layers and over top and sides of cake.

Bun's Restaurant
Delaware County

EXPLORE

Bun's Restaurant

14 West Winter Street • Delaware, OH 43015
740-363-2867 • www.bunsrestaurant.net

Bun's Restaurant celebrated its 150th anniversary in 2014, and was recognized as the oldest running business in Ohio. In all those years, there have only been three owners. The restaurant began with a bakery in 1864, and is still known for cut-out cookies and fudge cake. When meeting people who lived, visited or attended Ohio Wesleyan University in Delaware, the first thing they usually ask "Is Bun's still there?"

Big Apple Cake

1¼ cups oil
2 cups sugar
3 eggs
3 cups flour
1 teaspoon baking soda
1½ teaspoons cinnamon
½ teaspoon salt
3½ cups apples, chopped
2 teaspoons vanilla extract

Mix oil and sugar; add eggs 1 at a time, blending well after each. Sift dry ingredients together and add to mixture. Fold in apples and vanilla. Pour into greased 10-inch tube pan. Bake at 325° for approximately 1¼ hours, or until toothpick inserted comes out clean.

Note: Idared and Jonagold apples work extremely well, but different crunchy, somewhat tart apples should do.

Peg Vodraska, owner
Rittman Orchards & Farm Market

Rittman Orchards & Farm Market

13548 Mount Eaton Road • Doylestown, OH 44230
330-925-4152 • www.rittmanorchards.com
Find us on facebook, as well as twitter and Instagram @rittmanorchards

Rittman Orchard is a family-owned and operated fruit and vegetable farm located in the heart of northeast Ohio. They are best known for their over 65 apple varieties, but they grow many, many other things as well. Summer berries, peaches and plums, heirloom tomatoes and peppers, gourmet sweet corn and much more are grown on the farm and can all be found in season in the market.

Various family-oriented activities are available throughout the year. Summertime kicks off with pick-your-own strawberries, followed by raspberries and blueberries in midsummer. Fall brings pick-your-own apples and pumpkins. Complete your fall visit with a wagon ride around the orchard and a trip through the corn maze. Please visit their website or follow them on social media for hours, activities, and what's currently in season.

Williamsburg Orange Cake

2½ cups all-purpose flour or 2¼ cups cake flour
  (do not use self-rising flour)
1½ cups sugar
1½ teaspoons baking soda
¼ teaspoon salt
1½ cups buttermilk
½ cup margarine or butter, softened
¼ cup shortening
3 eggs
1½ teaspoons vanilla
1 cup chopped golden raisins
½ cup finely chopped nuts
1 tablespoon grated orange peel

Heat oven to 350°. Grease and flour a 9x13-inch pan or two 9-inch or three 8-inch round layer pans. Beat all ingredients in large mixer bowl on low speed, scraping bowl constantly, 30 seconds. Beat on high speed, scraping bowl occasionally, 3 minutes. Pour into pans. Bake until wooden pick inserted in center comes out clean, oblong 45 to 50 minutes, layers 30 to 35 minutes. Cool. Frost with Williamsburg Butter Frosting.

Williamsburg Butter Frosting:
½ cup margarine or butter, softened
4½ cups powdered sugar
4 to 5 tablespoons orange-flavored liqueur (or orange juice)
1 tablespoon grated orange peel

Beat margarine and powdered sugar with an electric mixer. Beat in liqueur/orange juice and orange peel. Spread over cake and/or between layers.

June in Olde Williamsburgh

June in Olde Williamsburgh

549 West Main Street
Williamsburg, OH 45176
513-724-6107
www.juneinoldewilliamsburgh.org

The June in Olde Williamsburgh Festival began as the Bicentennial celebration in 1996 but now, years later, the celebration continues to offer activities and entertainment for all ages. From the thrilling fun of carnival rides to the rockin' music on stage—there is some fun for everyone! A parade begins the festival 6pm on Friday evening, and there is live entertainment Friday and Saturday evenings from 6:45pm to midnight. During the entertainment there is a beer garden. There is a 5k/10k run Saturday morning, a Kids Fest on Saturday from 12pm to 2pm and a car show on Sunday morning. The shopping is terrific due to the fantastic vendors throughout the weekend. June in Olde Williamsburgh is a great time to visit with friends, relax on the lawn and listen to some music or just sit and enjoy the sights and the sounds of the festival.

Popcorn Cake

- 2 teaspoons plus ¼ cup vegetable oil, divided
- 12 cups popped popcorn, plain and unsalted
- 2 cups M&M's candy
- 1 cup lightly salted peanuts
- 1 stick unsalted butter
- 1 pound marshmallows

Grease a large tube or Bundt cake pan with 2 teaspoons oil and set aside. In a large bowl, mix popped corn with M&M's candy and peanuts. In a small saucepan melt butter, remaining ¼ cup oil and marshmallows over medium low heat, stirring occasionally. When melted, pour over popcorn mixture and stir to combine. Pour into prepared cake pan, pressing down to fit. Cover with aluminum foil to keep moist and let rest until firm, 3 to 4 hours. To serve, invert cake pan onto a large cake plate or platter. Shake gently to release. Serve at room temperature.

Note: Dried fruit such as pineapple, cherries, dates, raspberries, cranberries, and blueberries may be substituted for the nuts or M&M's. Dice fruit into small pieces. Instead of Bundt cake pan, try using a 9x13-inch pan.

Tom & Jill Becker
Wyandot Popcorn Museum

Marion County Historical Society

Wyandot Popcorn Museum

169 East Church Street • Marion, OH 43302
740-387-4255
www.marionhistory.com • www.wyandotpopcornmus.com

The Marion County Historical Society nurtures interest in history through special events, children's programming, and the Heritage Hall museum located in the former Marion post office. MCHS's Harding Presidential Collection chronicles the life and career of Marion's Warren G. Harding, 29th President of the United States. On the first Saturday of November each year, the society presents "Dinner with the Presidents" featuring re-enactors portraying past presidents of the United States. Along with meeting the presidents, participants enjoy a meal based on the presidential favorites chosen from recipes from White House cookbooks. Heritage Hall is also home to the world's largest collection of popcorn poppers and peanut roasters, all housed under a giant circus tent! Since 1982, the Wyandot Popcorn Museum has been a great place for families and kids of all ages to visit and delight in the experience of seeing the many ways one of America's favorite snacks has been made. Stop in for a poppin' good time!

Caramel Apple Cupcakes

3 cups flour
1 teaspoon baking soda
¼ teaspoon cinnamon
2 cups sugar
3 eggs
1½ cups vegetable oil
2 teaspoons pure vanilla extract
3 cups chopped Granny Smith apples
1 cup chopped walnuts

Combine dry ingredients. Add wet ingredients plus apples; mix well. Stir in nuts. Fill 32 standard-size cupcake liners approximately three-quarters full. Bake at 325° for approximately 19 minutes.

Caramel Butter Cream Icing:

¾ pound unsalted butter
1½ cups powdered sugar
5 tablespoons caramel sauce
6 tablespoons whole milk or cream

Soften and beat butter. Gradually add powdered sugar while mixing on slow. Half way through adding powdered sugar, add caramel sauce and milk/cream. Add remaining powdered sugar. Beat on medium speed until well blended. Spread on cooled cupcakes.

Sweet by Kristy

Downtown Tipp City

4 East Main Street, Suite 200
Tipp City, OH 45371
937-667-0883
www.downtowntippcity.org

Tipp City, Ohio, is a place where quality of life and small-town values still reside. Where excellence in education and community support is defined. Where businesses take pride in their products and services. Where history meets progress and growth. It's a small Midwestern town conveniently located minutes north of Dayton on I-75 and accessible along the Great Miami River Bikeway and Recreation Trail. Known throughout the region for its outstanding school system, charming historical business district, and family-friendly atmosphere, it is a unique community with an eclectic blend of history, shopping and exquisite dining experiences.

Red Velvet Whoopies

1 box red velvet cake mix
3 eggs
½ cup vegetable oil
½ cup water
½ cup flour

Combine ingredients and mix for 2 minutes. Drop by rounded spoonfuls onto a cookie sheet lined with parchment paper. Bake at 350° in a preheated oven 8 to 10 minutes.

Icing:

4 ounces cream cheese, softened
¼ cup butter, softened
1¼ cups powdered sugar
1 teaspoon vanilla

Beat cream cheese, butter and vanilla on low speed until well combined. Slowly add powdered sugar, beating on low speed until creamy. For each whoopie pie, spread icing on bottom of 1 cookie, then place second cookie bottom side down on icing. Refrigerate until set.

The Amish Door Village

The Amish Door Village

Stay. Dine. Shop. Relax.

1210 Winesburg Street • Wilmot, OH 44689
888-AMISHDOOR
www.amishdoor.com

Built like an oversized Amish home, the Amish Door Restaurant pays tribute to the Miller family's Amish-Mennonite heritage. Visit for breakfast, lunch or dinner for the finest in Amish-style cooking featuring an exceptional salad bar, the popular "Broasted" Chicken, homemade rolls, and real mashed potatoes.

Relax in the peace and quiet of Amish Country as the Inn at Amish Door provides a perfect getaway.

Stop in the Bakery for numerous fresh baked breads, pies, pastries and more. Visit shops where treasures abound, from ladies accessories and home décor, to bulk foods and deli items.

Pumpkin Chocolate Chip Cookies

1 cup canned pumpkin
1 cup sugar
½ cup vegetable oil
1 egg
2 cups flour
2 teaspoons baking powder
1½ teaspoons cinnamon
½ teaspoon salt
1 teaspoon baking soda
1 teaspoon milk
1 tablespoon vanilla
1 (11-ounce) bag chocolate chips

Combine pumpkin, sugar, vegetable oil and egg in a large bowl. In a separate bowl, stir together flour, baking powder, cinnamon and salt. Dissolve baking soda with milk and stir into wet ingredients. Add flour mixture to pumpkin mixture and mix well. Stir for about 1 minute. Add vanilla and chocolate chips and stir until combined. Line baking sheet with parchment paper. Drop cookies on by the spoonful. Bake at 350° for 10 to 12 minutes.

Kristin Leaders
Leaders Farms

ScreamAcres Haunted Cornfield

Leaders Farms

Home of The Maize and ScreamAcres Haunted Attraction

Located at State Route 24 and County Road 16 • Napoleon, OH 43545
419-599-1570
www.leadersfarms.com • www.screamacres.com

Open weekends in September and October.
Visit the website for dates and times.

The Leaders family has been entertaining guests on their farm for the past 18 years. A small pumpkin patch and a few school field trips have grown into a month and a half long fall festival.

The Leaders and the Maize group teamed up to make intricate maze designs including The Ohio Bicentennial, The War of 1812, The University of Toledo, and even a marriage proposal! And yes, she said yes! In 2013 the Leaders family added "Big Jack" the pumpkin cannon, which shoots pumpkins over 2100 feet several times a day during the season. Along with weekend festivities they offer school field trips during the week, which includes hayrides, jumping on the barnyard bouncer, education and much more. To add to the excitement of fall the Leaders Family has ScreamAcres Haunted Cornfield and The Pandemonium Project. As brave people make their way through the disorienting paths of corn they never know what is "stalking" them!

Maple Coconut Cookies

4 cups flour
1 teaspoon salt
¼ teaspoon baking soda
4 teaspoons baking powder
1 cup butter
1 cup brown sugar
1 cup maple syrup
2 eggs, well beaten
1 cup coconut flakes

Preheat oven to 350°. Sift flour, salt, baking soda and baking powder together in large mixing bowl. Cut in butter like making pastry. In separate bowl combine brown sugar, maple syrup and eggs. Mix wet ingredients into dry ingredients. Stir in coconut. Drop level tablespoons of dough onto cookie sheet and bake about 8 minutes, or until edges turn golden brown. Makes 6 dozen cookies.

Cincinnati Nature Center

Maple Pecan Cookies

⅔ cup butter
1 cup maple syrup
1 teaspoon vanilla
½ teaspoon salt
4 cups flour, divided
¾ cup finely chopped pecans
Pecan halves (if desired) and coarse white decorating sugar

Beat butter until smooth. Add maple syrup, vanilla, salt and 1 cup flour. Beat together. Continue adding remaining 3 cups flour 1 cup at a time and continue beating to make a stiff dough. Separate dough into 4 equal portions and roll each portion into a 7-inch log about 1½ inches in diameter. Place finely chopped pecans in pan or cookie sheet and roll each log into nuts, gently pushing nuts into dough. Wrap each log tightly in wax paper and refrigerate 2 hours or overnight. Preheat oven to 350°. With sharp knife, slice dough into ¼-inch thick rounds. Rotate log as you cut it to keep it from flattening. Place rounds on cookie sheet and lightly press pecan halves in middle of each cookie (if desired). Sprinkle cookie tops with coarse white sugar. Bake 7 to 8 minutes, or until edges turn golden brown. Makes about 6 dozen cookies.

Cincinnati Nature Center

Cincinnati Nature Center

4949 Tealtown Road • Milford, OH 45150
513-831-1711 • www.CincyNature.org

Just minutes away from the downtown urban core, Cincinnati Nature Center offers tranquility and solace among more than 1,600 acres of forests, fields, streams and ponds. With twenty miles of award-winning trails on two picturesque properties, the Nature Center provides spectacular experiences for people of all ages during all seasons. From enchanting spring wildflowers to the dazzling colors of autumn, the ever-changing beauty of nature attracts more than 150,000 visitors each year.

Cincinnati Nature Center provides the community with a unique and valuable education resource for innovative, nature-based learning opportunities in a variety of formats. School field trips, family and adult seasonal programming, summer camps, off-site travel, teacher retreats, in-school programs and volunteer classes all help connect individuals with nature. Some of our most popular programs feature late winter maple sugaring demonstrations and hand-crafted syrup production.

Viola Armstrong's Soft Molasses Drops

¾ cup butter
1½ cups brown sugar
3 eggs
1 teaspoon vanilla
2 tablespoons molasses
1 teaspoon baking soda
3 cups sifted flour
1 cup raisins

Cream butter and sugar until light and fluffy. Add eggs, 1 at a time, beating well after each addition. Beat in vanilla. Combine molasses and baking soda. Add to creamed mixture. Gradually add in flour. Add raisins. If you do not care for raisins just put 1 on the top. Drop by teaspoons onto greased baking sheet. Bake at 350° for 8 minutes or until brown. Remove from pan. Cool on racks.

Viola Armstrong, Neil Armstrong's Mother
Armstrong Air & Space Museum

Town of Wapakoneta

After visiting the museum, explore downtown Wapakoneta with its wonderful mix of unique, antique and specialty shops. Enjoy a tasty lunch and homemade fudge at Cloud Nine Café or admire the 1893 carved Brunswick back bar and delicious home cooking at the Alpha Cafe. You may also want to check out the Auglaize County Courthouse, a true architectural gem and end the day at casually elegant Marley's Downtown for great cuisine and specialty cocktails.

Armstrong Air & Space Museum

500 Apollo Drive
Wapakoneta, OH 45895
419-738-8811
www.armstrongmuseum.org

The Armstrong Air & Space Museum, located in Neil Armstrong's boyhood hometown of Wapakoneta, pays tribute to the first man on the moon and highlights the many Ohio Astronauts' contributions to space exploration. Among the items on display are an F5D Sky Lancer, Gemini VIII spacecraft, Apollo 11 artifacts and a moon rock. Learn about Armstrong's life and see how a young man from small town America became the first man to walk on the moon.

Sour Cream Apple Squares

2 cups flour
2 cups packed brown sugar
1 to 2 teaspoons cinnamon
½ cup butter, softened
1 cup nuts
1 teaspoon baking soda
½ teaspoon salt
1 cup sour cream
1 teaspoon vanilla
1 egg
2 cups peeled, finely chopped apples

In a large bowl combine first 4 ingredients. Blend at low speed until crumbly. Stir in nuts. Press 2¾ cups crumb mixture in ungreased 9x13-inch pan. Blend remaining crumbs and remaining ingredients, except apples. Stir in apples. Spoon evenly over base. Bake 25 to 35 minutes at 350°.

Apple Hill Orchards

Apple Hill Orchards

1175 Lex-Ontario Road • Mansfield, OH 44903
419-884-1500 • www.applehillorchards.com

Apple Hill Orchards is a family owned and operated orchard and farm market located in North Central Ohio. They grow apples, peaches, pears, plums and cherries, most of which are offered for pick-your-own in season. Cider is pressed on site, and there is an in-store bakery featuring cookies, pies, breads as well as the famous apple donuts. There is local maple syrup and honey, jams, jellies, candies, gift items and much more. There is an observation beehive and, in the fall, a resident goat and sheep for petting and feeding as well as a flock of chickens. In the fall the Farm offers pick-your-own pumpkins as well as apples, group/school tours, and special fall events including wagon tours, balloon man, pony rides, cider-pressing, tots' fun house and more.

Erie Monster Brownies

Brownie:

1 cup butter, softened
2 cups dark brown sugar
2 teaspoons vanilla extract
3 eggs
3 ounces unsweetened chocolate, melted
2 cups unsifted flour
1½ teaspoons baking powder
½ teaspoon salt
1 cup chopped nuts, optional

Preheat oven to 350°. In a large bowl, combine butter, brown sugar and vanilla; beat until creamy. Add eggs 1 at a time, beating well after each addition. Add melted chocolate and stir. Gradually blend in flour, baking powder and salt. Stir in nuts. Spread into well-greased 9x13-inch baking pan and bake 30 to 35 minutes. Cool.

Mint Frosting:

4 cups powdered sugar
1 cup butter, softened
3 tablespoons milk
1 teaspoon mint extract
Drop of green food coloring

Combine all frosting ingredients, mixing thoroughly. Spread over cooled brownie. Place in freezer for 15 to 20 minutes to harden the frosting. In the meantime prepare chocolate glaze.

Chocolate Glaze:

2 ounces unsweetened chocolate
2 tablespoons butter

Heat chocolate and butter in a small saucepan, blending thoroughly. When melted and combined, carefully pour over cooled, frosted brownie; tilt the pan if necessary to cover all the green frosting with the chocolate glaze.

Refrigerate until the glaze is set.

Maritime Museum of Sandusky

Maritime Museum of Sandusky

125 Meigs Street
Sandusky, OH 44870
419-624-0274
www.sanduskymaritime.org
Facebook: Maritime Museum of Sandusky

JUNE, JULY AND AUGUST:
Tuesday through Saturday 10am – 4pm • Sundays 12noon – 4pm
Closed Mondays.

SEPTEMBER THROUGH MAY:
Fridays and Saturdays 10am – 4pm • Sundays 12noon – 4pm
Closed on all major holidays.

Please call for group information and current admission prices.

The Maritime Museum of Sandusky was formed in 1993 to collect, preserve and interpret the maritime heritage from Port Clinton to Huron, including the Lake Erie islands, and south to Milan to include the shipbuilding industry that was located there. The Maritime Museum features interactive exhibits and educational programs on a large variety of Lake Erie Maritime topics, including the history of local boat-makers like Lyman and Matthews Boats, ice harvesting, wetlands, commercial fishing, passenger boats to the Lake Erie Islands and Cedar Point, shipwrecks, Sandusky's role in the Underground Railroad, and much more! The Museum also features a model boat building station and a nautical gift shop, making this a great family-friendly destination.

Covered Bridge Brownies

½ cup softened butter
1 cup sugar
1 (16-ounce) can Hershey's chocolate syrup
4 eggs
1 cup flour
1 cup chopped nuts, optional

Preheat oven to 350°. Cream together butter and sugar until fluffy; beat in syrup. Add eggs 1 at a time; beat in flour gradually. Fold in nuts. Pour into 9x13-inch baking dish. Bake 25 minutes.

Chocolate Chip Frosting:

½ cup butter
1½ cups sugar
⅓ cup evaporated milk
½ cup chocolate chips

In saucepan combine butter, sugar and evaporated milk. Bring to a boil and boil 1 to 2 minutes. Stir in chocolate chips and stir until melted. Pour over brownies that just came out of the oven and spread quickly.

Union County Covered Bridge Bluegrass Festival

Union County Covered Bridge Bluegrass Festival

Third weekend in September

17141 Inskeep-Cratty Road • North Lewisburg, OH 43060
937-642-6279 • www.CoveredBridgeFestival.com

The annual Union County Covered Bridge Bluegrass Festival provides the entire family a chance to celebrate simpler times. At the Pottersburg Bridge, one of Union County's eight covered bridges, the festival captures the alluring sights, sounds and flavors of bygone days when covered bridges were more than a way to cross over water. Come experience an elegant sunset dinner on the Pottersburg Bridge, breakfast on the bridge, bluegrass music, horse-drawn wagon rides, bridge tours, a variety of food and artisan vendors, a pie baking contest, demonstrations of the 19th century craftsmanship, a community church service and so much more!

Phoebe's Cherry Delight

Crust:

2 cups graham cracker crumbs, crushed
2 sticks butter, melted

Mix together and press into 9x13-inch pan.

Filling:

1 cup powdered sugar
1 (8-ounce) block cream cheese, softened
2 (8-ounce) containers Cool Whip, divided
1 (20-ounce) can cherry pie filling

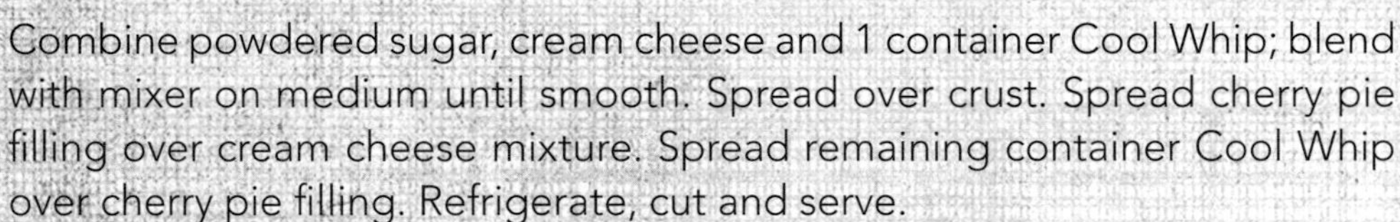

Combine powdered sugar, cream cheese and 1 container Cool Whip; blend with mixer on medium until smooth. Spread over crust. Spread cherry pie filling over cream cheese mixture. Spread remaining container Cool Whip over cherry pie filling. Refrigerate, cut and serve.

Appalachian Festival

Appalachian Festival

Mother's Day weekend in May

Coney Island Amusement Park

6201 Kellogg Avenue • Cincinnati, OH 45230

513-251-3378 • www.appalachianfestival.org

The Appalachian Festival is a celebration of heritage featuring, music, crafts, storytelling, educational history, demonstrations and great food for all who attend. The festival's mission is to help provide education and food to residents of Appalachia who are in need, especially children. Please search the web at Appalachian Festival Cincinnati for more information, and come join the celebration every Mother's Day weekend at the Coney Island amusement park in Cincinnati, Ohio.

Strawberry Mousse with Fresh Strawberries

1 (.25-ounce) envelope unflavored gelatin
1 cup strawberries, de-leafed
1 cup cream cheese
Juice of 1 lemon
¼ cup sugar
2 eggs whites

Melt gelatin according to package directions. Place two thirds of the strawberries in blender. Blend until smooth. Add cream cheese, lemon juice and sugar and process 15 more seconds. Add melted gelatin carefully to strawberry mixture. Place in refrigerator until mousse starts to gel. Beat egg whites and gently fold into strawberry mousse. Refrigerator for several hours. To serve, spoon into dessert dishes. Top each with 2 whole strawberries. Serves 4.

Newark Strawberry Festival

Weekend after Memorial Day

Newark, OH 43055

740-983-4797 • www.newarkstrawberryfestival.com

The Newark Strawberry Festival has become the largest festival held in Licking County each year. Visitors travel from all over Ohio and surrounding States to enjoy 3 days of amusement rides, games, crafts, food, musical entertainment, a queen's pageant, and the "World Famous Strawberry Shortcake". Each year, Newark Kiwanis Club members and volunteers gather on the eve of the festival to begin preparing enough strawberries to serve over 1500 delicious shortcakes. In addition, the shortcakes can be topped with a choice of vanilla or strawberry ice cream made locally by The Velvet Ice Cream Company at Ye Olde Mill in Utica, located just 9 miles north of Newark. The festival is always held the weekend after Memorial Day, so make plans to join the celebration of nature's sweetheart...the strawberry. Please call for detailed annual information.

Berry Whip

1¼ cups chopped berries (strawberries or raspberries)
1 cup powdered sugar
1 egg white
Lady fingers

Combine all ingredients except lady fingers; beat with a wire whisk until stiff enough to hold shape. Pile lightly on dish and chill. Surround with lady fingers and serve with the soft custard. Also delicious served with angel food cake, either as a frosting or sauce.

Ellen Gillespie, On the Road, the Women's Committee of the Crawford Auto and Aviation Museum
The Western Reserve Historical Society

The Western Reserve Historical Society History Center in University Circle

10825 East Boulevard • Cleveland, OH 44106
216-721-5722 • www.wrhs.org

Tuesday through Saturday 10am to 5pm • Sunday 12pm to 5pm

The Western Reserve Historical Society (WRHS) is Northeast Ohio's premier storyteller of history. WRHS works to inspire people to discover the American experience through the tangible history found in its vast and diverse collections. The 7-acre complex that comprises the History Center is home to the Crawford Auto-Aviation Museum, Research Library, Chisholm Halle Costume Wing, Euclid Beach Park Grand Carousel, two historic mansions, and rotating history exhibits.

Admission is $10.00 for adults, $9.00 for seniors, and $5.00 for students.
WRHS members and children 2 and younger are admitted for free.

Hamburger Inn Cinnamon Roll Bread Pudding

2 loaves cinnamon bread or cinnamon rolls
12 eggs
3 cups sugar, divided
2 tablespoons vanilla
3 quarts milk
1 pound salted butter, softened
4 cups 35 to 40% heavy cream

Cut cinnamon bread or cinnamon rolls in ½- to ¾-inch pieces. Spread pieces in 2-inch hotel pan or large roasting pan; fill almost to top. Leave some room, mixture will rise as it cooks. Combine eggs and 1 cup sugar with vanilla and milk; mix well. Pour mixture over bread pieces, make sure bread is saturated. Cover tightly with plastic wrap and foil and refrigerate overnight. When ready to cook, remove plastic wrap and replace foil to cover. Bake at 350° for 1 hour. Remove from oven and uncover, then bake an additional 10 minutes to brown the top.

Vanilla Cream Sauce Topping:

Blend butter, remaining sugar and cream in a saucepan. Bring to a simmer. If needed, thicken with a slurry of cornstarch and water. Serve warm or at room temperature. Spoon on top of bread pudding. Cut bread pudding into serving pieces and plate with cinnamon and brown sugar.

Hamburger Inn
Delaware County

Hamburger Inn

16 North Sandusky Street • Delaware, OH 43015
740-369-3850 • www.facebook.com/thehamburgerinn

The Hamburger Inn has been located in Historic Downtown Delaware since 1932. This old-fashioned countertop restaurant still serves hand-crafted milkshakes and food hot off the grill. The Hamburger Inn is famous for its fresh giant maple cinnamon rolls, baked buns and breads, gourmet hamburgers, and breakfast. The restaurant also serves a mean chili that students at Ohio Wesleyan University used to send home on dry ice.

PHOTO BY JENNIFER WAUGH PRICE

Apple Fritters

1 cup flour
¼ teaspoon salt
½ teaspoon nutmeg
1 egg, slightly beaten
1 cup milk
1 tablespoon melted fat
2 large apples, cored, pared and sliced
Fat for frying
Powdered sugar

Combine flour, salt, nutmeg; mix well and set aside. In separate bowl, combine egg, milk and fat; beat well. Gradually add to flour mixture. Mix with hand beater until blended. Chill batter for 30 minutes, it sticks to fruit better. Dip apples in batter and deep-fry. Sprinkle with powdered sugar and serve.

Yankee Peddler Festival

Yankee Peddler Festival

Held every year on the three weekends following Labor Day
Gates open at 10:30am and close at 6:00pm

Clays Park Resort

13190 Patterson Street NW • North Lawrence, OH 44666
800-535-5634 • www.yankeepeddlerfestival.com
Facebook: www.facebook.com/pages/Yankee-Peddler
Twitter: www.twitter.com/YPFestivals

Called "Our Fourteenth Colony" by *Western Reserve Magazine*, the Yankee Peddler Festival recreates life in pioneer Ohio of 1776–1825. The Festival combines the natural beauty of 75 acres of wooded glades separated by softly-flowing streams with the artistic beauty of the rustic shops set up around each bend by over 200 artists and artisans. Guests will enjoy happy, foot-stomping sounds of old-time bands, delicious aromas and foods all prepared over open fires, theatre productions, wandering magicians, and flag-raising by the militia and mountain men. Selected as the top "Traditional Show" in the nation by *Sunshine Magazine* and featured in the *Rand-McNally Ultimate Road Atlas & Vacation Guide*, Yankee Peddler has hosted more than two million visitors in its 43-year history. People come from all around to sample the apple fritters, funnel cakes, grilled meats, roasted corn, and food fare not to be found anywhere else.

Buckeyes

1½ cups creamy peanut butter
½ cup butter, softened
1 teaspoon vanilla extract
½ teaspoon salt
3 to 4 cups powdered sugar, divided
2 cups semisweet chocolate chips
2 tablespoons vegetable shortening

Combine peanut butter, butter, vanilla and salt in large bowl. Mix with blender on low until blended. Add 2 cups powdered sugar, beating on low until blended. Beat in additional powdered sugar until when a small amount of the mixture is shaped into a ball it is stiff enough to remain on a toothpick. Shape into 1-inch peanut butter balls and refrigerate. Place chocolate chips and shortening in microwave-safe bowl. Microwave 30 seconds, stir, repeat until mixture is smooth. Reheat as needed. Be careful not to overheat. Line a cookie sheet in wax paper. Insert toothpick in peanut butter ball. Dip three quarters into chocolate. Leave enough uncovered on top to resemble a buckeye. Allow excess chocolate from the peanut butter ball to remain in bowl. Place on wax paper. Refrigerate until firm.

Paula Williams-Wray
Gallia County Convention and Visitors Bureau

Gallia County Convention and Visitors Bureau

441 Second Avenue • Gallipolis, OH 45631
740-446-6882 • www.visitgallia.com

Welcome to Gallia County, Ohio!

Gallia County is honored to have visitors and take great strides so that each person visiting the area has a great experience. The sense of pride shared by Gallia's residents is contagious, and there are many attractions, events and other opportunities for visitors, family and friends to experience and enjoy. The Gallia County Visitor Guide offers a handy pocket-guide to the most popular and historic hot-spots with references to facility services and contact information to make sure needed information is readily available. Gallia County CVB's professional staff partners with various organizations that are prepared to respond to unique needs and to ensure an enriching experience.

Great things are happening in Gallia County, Ohio so be sure to check out their website at www.VisitGallia.com or download the free mobile app VisitGallia to keep up-to-date on the latest information!

Peanut Butter and Chocolate Fudge

3 cups sugar
¾ cup (1½ sticks) butter or margarine
⅔ cup evaporated milk
1 cup (generous) peanut butter or 1 (12-ounce) package semi-sweet chocolate chips
1 (7-ounce) jar marshmallow crème
1 teaspoon vanilla

Heat sugar, butter and evaporated milk to full rolling boil in a 3-quart heavy saucepan over medium heat, stirring constantly. Boil, stirring constantly (very important), for 5 minutes. Remove from heat. Stir in peanut butter (or chocolate) and marshmallow crème until melted; stir in vanilla. (Optional: stir in 1 cup chopped nuts for chocolate.) Spread immediately in treated 9x11-inch sheet pan. Cool at room temperature 1 to 2 hours. Cut into 1-inch squares. Makes 3 pounds.

Jim Weaver
Trains of Williamsburg Christmas Walk

Trains of Williamsburg Christmas Walk

First Friday of December

Williamsburg Village
Williamsburg, OH 45176
513-724-6107
www.williamsburgohio.org

Hours: 5:00 pm to 9:00 pm
Outdoor Event, Free

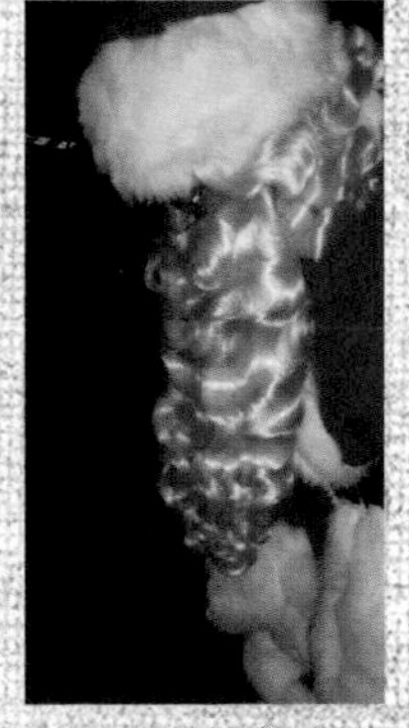

The Trains of Williamsburg Christmas Walk takes place the First Friday in December each year. The Christmas Walk is a free, family-friendly, outdoor event for which the businesses of Williamsburg open their doors after normal business hours, offering train displays, refreshments and holiday shopping. In addition to our local businesses and many train displays throughout the Village, you will find strolling carolers, firetruck rides, Santa Claus, music from local groups, and much more. Each year the committee holds a free raffle for a model train set that is donated in memory of a beloved train enthusiast. Entry for the raffle is free and fun, just visit the designated "conductor stops" and get your card stamped, turn it in and enjoy Williamsburg while you wait for the drawing at the end of the evening. Please stop in for an evening of fun for the family.

Caramel Chocolate Squares

1 (14-ounce) package caramels
1 (5-ounce) can evaporated milk, divided
1 package German chocolate cake mix
⅔ cup melted butter
¾ cup coarsely chopped walnuts or pecans
½ (12-ounce) package semi-sweet chocolate chips
1 cup flaked coconut

Heat oven to 350°. Heat caramels and ¼ cup milk in a saucepan over medium heat, stirring constantly until caramels are melted and mixture is smooth. Keep warm over low heat, stirring occasionally. Combine cake mix, butter, remaining milk and nuts; mix well. Spread half of dough in ungreased 9x13-inch pan. Bake 6 minutes and remove from oven. Sprinkle with chocolate chips and coconut. Drizzle caramel mixture over chocolate chips and coconut. Drop remaining dough by teaspoonfuls over layer, spreading evenly. (If mixture gets too cool, run a spatula under hot water to help spread the mixture more evenly.) Bake until cake portion is slightly dry to touch, 15 to 20 minutes longer. Cool completely. Refrigerate until firm. Cut into squares to serve.

Alpacas of Spring Acres

Index

Ohio State Flower *Dianthus caryophyllus*

Index of Events & Destinations

H

J

K

Y

Z

Index of Recipes

B

C

D

E

K

L

M

N

O

P

R

S

T

V

W

Y

Z

About the Author

In 1999, Christy Campbell began her journey in the world of cookbooks when she took a position at a publishing company specializing in regional cookbooks. At the time, it was an all-new experience, so she immersed herself in cookbooks, both at home and at the office. With the help of the associate publisher and her personal mentor, Sheila Simmons (author, STATE HOMETOWN COOKBOOK SERIES), Christy learned the in's and out's of the small press world, devoting herself to cookbooks for the next 6 years. After the birth of her youngest son, Campbell took a sabbatical from the publishing world to focus on her young family.

In 2009, Campbell reconnected with Sheila Simmons and began work with Great American Publishers, reenergizing a 10 year love of cookbooks. She is now an integral part of Great American Publishers and has begun a new cookbook series of her own. The EAT & EXPLORE STATE COOKBOOK SERIES chronicles the favorite recipes of local cooks across the United States while highlighting the most popular events and destinations in each state.

When she is not writing cookbooks, selling cookbooks or cooking recipes for cookbooks, Christy Campbell enjoys volunteering at her children's school, running and reading. She lives in Brandon, Mississippi, with her husband Michael and their two sons.

More Great American Cookbooks

State Hometown Cookbook Series

A Hometown Taste of America, One State at a Time.

Each state's charm is revealed through local recipes from resident cooks along with stories and photos that will take you back to your hometown . . . or take you on a journey to explore other hometowns across the country.

EACH: $18.95 • 256 pages • 8x9 • paperbound

Georgia • Louisiana • Mississippi • South Carolina
Tennessee • Texas • West Virginia

State Back Road Restaurants Series

Every road leads to delicious food.

From two-lane highways and interstates, to dirt roads and quaint downtowns, every road leads to delicious food when traveling across our United States. Each well-researched and charming guide leads you to the state's best back road restaurants. No time to travel? No problem. Each restaurant shares their favorite recipes—sometimes their signature dish, sometimes a family favorite, always delicious.

EACH: $18.95 • 256 pages • 7x9 • paperbound • full-color

Alabama • Kentucky • Tennessee • Texas

It's So Easy…

Kitchen Memories Cookbook

Your Recipe for Family Fun in the Kitchen

This kids' cookbook and free-style memory book guarantees hours of fun and a lifetime of memories for your family. It's a cookbook, a memory book, and an activity book—all in one! A cherished keepsake for your family.

Family Favorite Recipes

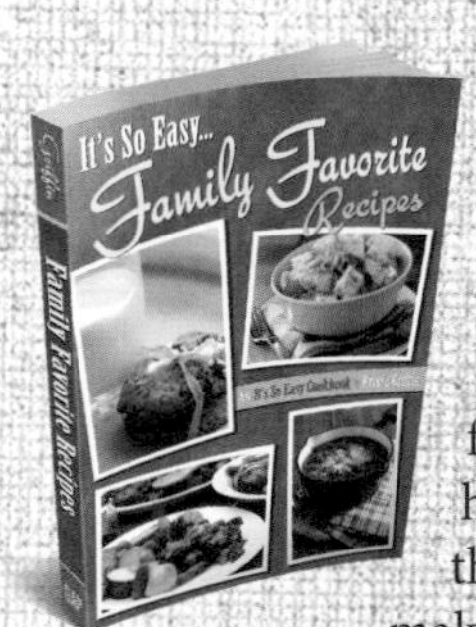

It's so easy to cook great food your family will love with 350 simply delicious recipes for easy-to-afford, easy-to-prepare dinners. It's so easy to encourage your family to eat more meals at home…to enjoy time spent in the kitchen… to save money making delicious affordable meals…to cook the foods your family loves without the fuss…with Family Favorite Recipes.

EACH: $18.95 • 248 pages • 7x10 • paperbound • full-color

www.GreatAmericanPublishers.com • www.facebook.com/GreatAmericanPublishers

Eat & Explore Cookbook Series

Discover community celebrations and unique destinations, as they share their favorite recipes.

Arkansas ***Minnesota*** ***Ohio*** ***Oklahoma***

This series is a favorite of local cooks, armchair travelers, and cookbook collectors across the nation.

Explore the distinct flavor of each state by savoring 200 favorite local recipes. In addition, fun festivals, exciting events, unique attractions, and fascinating tourist destinations are profiled throughout the book with everything you need to plan your family's next getaway.

EACH: $18.95 • 256 pages
7x9 • paperbound

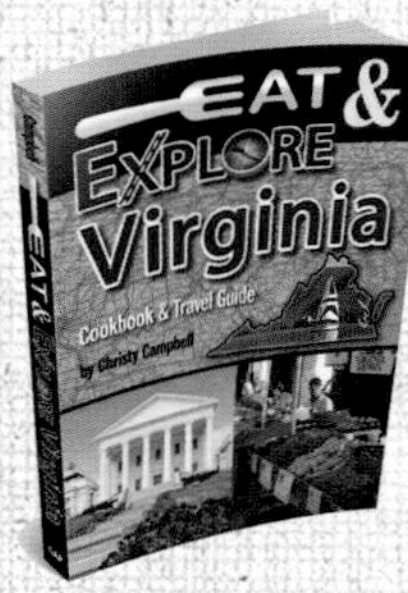

North Carolina ***Virginia*** ***Washington***

ORDER FORM

Mail to: Great American Publishers • 501 Avalon Way • Brandon, MS 39047
Or call us toll-free 1.888.854.5954 to order by check or credit card

o Check Enclosed

Charge to: o Visa o MC o AmEx o Disc

Card # ____________________

Exp Date Signature ____________________

Name ____________________

Address ____________________

City/State ____________________

Zip ____________________

Phone ____________________

Email ____________________

Qty.	Title	Total
	Subtotal	
	Postage ($4.00 first book; $1.00 each additional; Order 4 or more books, FREE SHIPPING)	
	Total	